Cathie Ostapchuk is a Canadian voice to listen to, a national leader of uncommon wisdom, deeply committed to faithfully passing on the torch of faith to the next generation. Read these pages and feel the marrow in your bones ignite with bold courage!

—Ann Voskamp
New York Times bestselling author
The Broken Way and *One Thousand Gifts*

In *Brave Women, Bold Moves,* Cathie Ostapchuk gives women (and men, if you are reading, and you should!) a portal into the larger narrative arc that historically and biblically elevates and affirms the significance of women as catalysts in moving the story of God forward. If you want to lead from a place of courage in a world that pressures to conform, this is for you.

—Carey Nieuwhof
bestselling author
founder pastor, Connexus Church

Cathie has written a book that should encourage every woman to choose to walk each day in the purpose God has intended for them. Too often, it is easy to shirk back. But, with examples of women from scripture who said "yes" to each prompting of the Spirit, Cathie encourages women to do the same and follow their example. God has plans for each woman, and taking the steps to obediently walk with Him is not always without fear or questions. This book will encourage women to walk with God, and understand that His story of redemption and grace flows through those He calls to His glory and praise.

—Dr. Pamela MacRae
Professor of Applied Theology and Church Ministry Department
Program Head of Ministry to Women
and Ministry to Victims of Sexual Exploitation
Moody Bible Institute
Chicago, IL

Brave Women, Bold Moves offers fresh, deep, and relevant insights into the lives of women from the Bible, infused with rugged authenticity and fearless honesty! Cathie shares from her own experience of the real-life struggle as a woman of faith in today's world. She brings these stories to life with the audacious hope of bringing you to life as well!

—Danielle Strickland
author of *The Liberating Truth*
founder of Boundless Communications, Inc.
as well as Brave Global, Amplify Peace,
Infinitum, and Women Speaker Collective initiatives

We need to push the reset button on the role of women in the church. For too long, the church has elevated the voices of only one half of the image of God in our mission of sharing the good news of Jesus. Thank you, Cathie, for encouraging women to step into the line of biblical women who have bravely chosen to use their gifts for God, whatever the cost.

—Bruxy Cavey
teaching pastor at The Meeting House
author of *The End of Religion* and *"(re)union"*

When your back is against the wall, be brave. The Bible says, "We can do all things through Christ Jesus who strengthens us!" Pray, and the Holy Spirit will guide your steps. *Brave Women, Bold Moves* is a must-read. Be inspired!

—Joy Smith, B.Ed., M.Ed., O.M.
former Member of Parliament
founder and president, Joy Smith Foundation

The mind wars of doubt are paralyzing. Cathie shares her own life experiences to encourage each reader how to be bold and brave, and how choosing to be courageous can be a catalyst to reaching your God-written destiny.

—Anne Miranda
Bible teacher
Director of Women's Ministries, Village Church Canada
co-founder of Leverage, a network of Women in Leadership

Brave Women, Bold Moves captured my imagination and inspired me again to live brave. Cathie gives a rally cry to all women to rise up! To be brave! She takes you on a journey through the biblical narrative, giving you a closer look at real women, in real time, learning to be brave. This is a much-needed message. This book will make you brave! I highly recommend it.

—Lorie Hartshorn
co-host, 700 Club Canada
speaker, leadership consultant
and author of *Finding Freedom* Bible study

If you're looking for inspiration and a big dose of bravery to launch yourself towards the destiny God has for you, then *Brave Women, Bold Moves* is a must-read. What a deep breath of fresh air to walk hand-in-hand through the biblical narrative from the perspective of the women who lived it. I highly recommend it!

—Cheryl Weber
co-host and senior executive producer, "100 Huntley Street"

Brave Women, Bold Moves is a thoughtful work that offers the guardrails for deep reflection to keep you from the pitfalls that often attend those in search of their authentic voice. Biblical, humble, and insightful, Cathie Ostapchuk offers surrogate courage until you find your own.

—Stacey Campbell
president and CEO
Prison Fellowship Canada

A fair warning before reading this book: You're about to engage in a brave and courageous life. Cathie Ostapchuk's inspiration comes directly from God's heart and He is speaking personally to each and every one of you. You will be shaken to your core and be unable to resist God's calling.

—Stephanie Reader, Ph.D.
author, speaker and pastor
Église Nouvelle Vie
Montreal, Canada

Brave Women, Bold Moves carries a timely and important message that will resonate deep within the heart of every reader. Cathie Ostapchuk invites us to explore the lives of some of the brave women of the Bible as she opens up her own journey of making bold moves into unexplored, exciting territory with God. This book is an excellent guide and resource to encourage you to venture further and deeper into all that God has designed for your life. The world is waiting for women to rise up with bravery and boldness for such a time as this.

—Helen Burns
founding and teacher pastor at Relate Church, Surrey, BC
Hillsong channel TV host, "Sex, Love, and Relationships"

Every reader is sure to be both inspired and ignited to step into the bold moments of their lives and do the brave things God has called them to, with this must-read book! Cathie Ostapchuk's biblical teaching on bravery is deeply insightful, enlightening, and life-changing. This is a book desperately needed in this time.

—Cheryl Nembhard
author of *Brave: This Is Us*
founder of Exousia Media Group and The Lighthouse Project
and co-host of "See, Hear, Love"

Cathie lives out the words on these pages. These are not stories removed from our reality; these are invitations that say, "I am understood" and when I read of the life of these biblical women, I found myself within her. Her words are the same as her voice when you are with Cathie... true, authentic, meaningful, and powerful. She is a champion of womanhood in all her glorious expressions. Thank you for YOUR bravery!

—Vanessa Hoyes
speaker, coach, and pastor
Resurgent Church, Montreal

By simply pausing, reading, and pondering the words on these pages, you are brave. Throughout each chapter are biblical stories and everyday stories of bravery with raw, authentic, and vulnerable expressions. Step out of your comfort zone, into the danger zone—one that provides a front-row seat to the new brave adventure that awaits you and me. And, invite a friend or two to join you!

—Alana Walker Carpenter
CEO, Intriciti

It is an honour to be one of those who endorse *Brave Women, Bold Moves: Choosing Courage in a Culture of Conformity,* written by Cathie Ostapchuk, one of my finest graduate students in over fifty years of teaching. Despite a tight schedule, I could not put down the manuscript until it was read cover to cover. Cathie's presentation of the challenge of being brave women who lead is so essential in the 21st century.

The crafting of the challenging story with her own story with vulnerability, the vulnerability of significant women she invited to share theirs, the depth of biblical research and reporting on the lives of women of biblical history has produced a goldmine of value for women of all ages and seasons. Indeed, an awesome resource for both men and women who wish to gain a deepened understanding of the challenge women have to recognize that God is able and God is God in their pursuit of a brave life that moves us through fear to step into bold moments, messages, manners, and modelling that impacts the trajectory of history and generations to come. Congratulations, Cathie.

—Paul Magnus, Ph.D.
President Emeritus, Distinguished Chair and
Professor of Leadership/Management, Briercrest Seminary
Caronport, Saskatchewan
coach, consultant, facilitator

BRAVE
WOMEN
BOLD
MOVES

Choosing Courage in a Culture of Conformity

CATHIE OSTAPCHUK

BRAVE WOMEN, BOLD MOVES
Copyright © 2019 by Cathie Ostapchuk

Scripture quotations labelled (NLT) are taken from the Holy Bible, New Living Translation, copyright ©1996, 2004, 2007 by Tyndale House Foundation. Used by permission of Tyndale House Publishers, Inc., Carol Stream, Illinois 60188. All rights reserved. Scripture quotations labelled (NIV) are taken from the Holy Bible, NEW INTERNATIONAL VERSION®, NIV® Copyright © 1973, 1978, 1984, 2011 by Biblica, Inc.® Used by permission. All rights reserved worldwide. Scripture quotations labelled (ESV) are taken from The Holy Bible, English Standard Version® (ESV®), copyright © 2001 by Crossway, publishing ministry of Good News Publishers. Used by permission. All rights reserved. Scripture quotations labelled (AMP) are taken from the Amplified® Bible (AMP), Copyright © 2015 by The Lockman Foundation. Used by permission. www.Lockman.org Scripture quotations labelled (AMPC) are taken from the Amplified® Bible, Copyright © 1954, 1958, 1962, 1964, 1965, 1987 by The Lockman Foundation. Used by permission. www.Lockman.org

Printed in Canada

Print ISBN: 978-1-4866-1902-3
eBook ISBN: 978-1-4866-1903-0

Word Alive Press
119 De Baets Street, Winnipeg, MB R2J 3R9
www.wordalivepress.ca

MIX
Paper from
responsible sources
FSC® C016245

Cataloguing in Publication may be obtained through Library and Archives Canada

*For my brave and beautiful daughters and daughter-in-love,
Tasha, Halina, and Laura, and to my never-to-be forgotten mom,
Nettie, who was a woman ahead of her time.*

*To anyone who has felt the oppressive fear of living up to society's
expectations to feel valued: you are seen and you are loved. You
have inherent value because you are a Daughter of God. You have
a remarkable opportunity to influence future generations if you
are willing to choose courage.*

Your brave is now.

CONTENTS

ACKNOWLEDGEMENTS

There really is no greater truth than that He makes me brave. There would be no courage in my heart if God had not placed it there because of His grace. I am so grateful that He went first and made His brave move to rescue me from all that would have kept me imprisoned in fear.

I heard God's strong and tender voice calling me to ministry in this nation: "Find your voice, and help others find theirs." I am eternally grateful for the caster of courage, the giver of brave voice, and Creator of all.

I also want to acknowledge the brave men in my world: my husband, Stephen, my son, Jordan, my son-in-law James Allen, who designed the beautiful, bold cover of this book, and my warrior grandsons, Archer Walter Brawn, Jake Atlas, and Hendrix Montgomery.

In addition, I want to thank each woman who offered a stunning snippet of her brave story in this book. Thank you to:

- Joanna Lafleur, speaker, podcaster, digital consultant (joannalafleur.com)
- Vanessa Hoyes, pastor, coach (vanessahoyes.com)
- Jennie Nadeau, Teen Challenge Canada staff, speaker
- Kallie Wood, Nakota Cree of Carry the Kettle Nakoda First Nation, owner at convergingpathways.ca
- Bonnie Pue, blogger, pastor, co-founder at theunionmovement.com

I hold you all in such high regard and honour your voices in your unique spheres of influence.

We are never meant to do this journey alone. I have had the privilege of being mentored, loved, and encouraged in my life and leadership journey by incredible women. Lynn Smith modelled what it was like to give away power by empowering me. She was Dean at Tyndale University, a brilliant author and leadership trainer, and yet she always made me feel like the smart one and my confidence soared under her loving guidance.

Eleanor Henderson poured into my life early on and throughout my marriage, and taught me that my most important sphere of influence were the people living under my roof. Both of these women continue to lavish the beautiful fragrance of their gifts on others with humility and warrior-like strength.

Thank you also to all of the women with whom I've had the privilege of connecting through Gather Women. I value each brave voice that graced the Gather Women platform across the nation and shared their poignant and powerful stories of grace and courage. Some of the "I Am and the Woman I Represent" moments, during which you shared your brave, undid me. You are all brave—each and every one of you. As you choose your brave moments, I know you'll have an impact on women in this nation and beyond.

You are loved!

WHERE DOES BRAVERY EVER GET YOU?

I used to picture myself as the brave woman in James Bond movies, either speeding down a glorious Mediterranean oceanside highway in an exotic sports car, or zipping down the ski hill in my glamorous one-piece ski outfit, hair waving, leaning into the curves. I was so confident that I would not only outrace everyone, but "get the man" doing it.

That was before I fell. And fell *hard*.

For someone who thought she was the brave one, I have often been the coward instead. I dreamt of being brave, but left a lot on the table when it came to speaking my brave words or acting with bold moves.

I tried so hard to follow everyone else's brave, and spent years avoiding unpacking what brave looked like for me. I hid behind an identity of performing for and pleasing people, slowly losing my voice and finding reasons to stay hidden. There was a time when I couldn't cope with the gap between who I was and who I wanted to be.

So I decided to throw in the towel.

It's only by God's grace I didn't succeed.

Where does bravery ever get you?

How would you answer that question right now? Maybe, like I did, you're looking around you and wondering for whom this question is meant. It must be for that smart, entrepreneurial woman starting her own online business, or the gifted one you see speaking on the platform, or the super-powered homeschooling mom of five who lives next door, or the one leading the women's ministry at church. *Those* are the brave ones. Surely this question isn't meant for *you*, right?

Oh, friend, it is—it most certainly is.

Perhaps you feel pain, doubt, or shame because you sense a call to step out of your ordinary life but can't envision the extraordinary journey that awaits you. It scares you.

And so it should.

I never wanted to have just an ordinary life. I tried to create those extraordinary moments for myself. Most of the time, I bombed. I wasn't making choices out of courage; I was making choices out of a need to be loved and wanting to be the same as everyone else. I wanted to conform to what I thought others wanted me to be. I performed myself to death, not realizing that brave without blessing turns to burnout.

If these words are hitting a nerve, then this book is written just for you; it's no accident that you're here. I want you to be encouraged by every word. I believe it's your destiny that your story confidently finds its place in God's story. Open the door with me to what it might mean to be brave, as we look at the lives of brave women who came before you and are around you right now. Be inspired to choose courage for all the girls coming after you.

As a young girl, I remember learning about biblical women in Sunday school—women with strange-to-me lives, including the young mother who dropped her basketed baby in the Nile River, or the "ancient" woman who miraculously delivered her first baby when she was older than my grandmother. Their lives didn't seem brave or even real—just very peculiar.

Sarah, Abraham's wife, got the occasional shout-out from the pulpit, but only in context of her relationship to her husband, the starring role as the receiver of God's covenant. I remember more about the men whose stories take up much of the Old Testament, men like Noah, Moses, and Abraham. "Women's invisibility is an age-old problem."[1]

Biblical women lived completely different lives in completely different times, I rationalized, so there was a disconnect between their other-worldly lives and my ordinary Canadian, middle-class, churchgoing life. They were merely mentioned in the Bible, not key players. I believed their roles were meant to be downplayed, hidden.

Or so I thought.

If you're like me, you might've placed some distance between your life and the lives of women who lived so long before you. Perhaps you, too, wrote them off as "just Bible story characters" with little to no relevance to your life. Perhaps they seemed larger than life, and you've found it difficult to imagine yourself in their situation. Perhaps, like me, you didn't consider them to be *real* women living *real* lives and often facing *real* danger.

Personally, I never imagined myself in the story of Moses' mother, who had to defy authority, weave a basket of surrender, place her precious son in it, and drop it in the Nile. I couldn't draw the lines between her life and my own experience, and I believed that somehow, it must have been easier for her because she knew that somehow everything would work out.

Except that she *didn't* know it would be okay. She had *no idea* where her bravery would get her.

She didn't know whether Moses would live or die. She certainly didn't know that I would be reading her story and be inspired to make my own bold moves thousands of years later.

Jochebed's bravery got her a mention in God's bigger story, and led to the ransom of a people from enslavement. And there are more women like her.

I believe *you* could be one of those women.

Not every woman chose well, but all were marked with grace. They were a mix of holy and harlot, faithful and failures, too "old" and too "naïve": mothers, wives, daughters-in-law, widows, and foreigners, and often the least likely to get a mention in God's story. And yet, there they were, showing up in the pages of both Testaments with stories that sound like modern-day soap operas full of drama, intrigue, truth and lies, deceit, despair, courage, and confidence.

What are we to make of their stories? Why were they included for us to read centuries later?

When I had daughters who became women, I wondered how closely they related to these fascinating-yet-distant biblical women. Were my girls' lives at all affected by the women's lives in Scripture?

I decided to dig into these incredible stories to study and gain an understanding of what made them so unique that they were given a place in the telling of the history of God and His people.

I was awestruck.

I realized I hadn't given these women enough credit. When I tried to imagine myself in their place and wondered what I would do in their circumstances, I realized my life was nowhere near as challenging and full of complexity as theirs. From Eve to Mary, I recognized that none of these women had easy choices to make.

And yet almost all of them *chose to be brave*, despite *not knowing* where their bravery would get them. "These women were edgy; they had dignity and character informed by knowledge. And when they suffered, that knowledge of God deepened."[2]

What's unique about their courageous actions? I believe that their brave moments were forged in character-defining choices of obedience to God. They all could have easily chosen to abandon their faith, and I would've understood, because their context left them very little room to maneuver. In many cases, their backs were quite literally up against the wall, and they didn't have a "sisterhood" around them to cheer them on, or a supportive political, social, or religious environment.

I have often felt like my back has been up against a wall. So I made excuses for my lack of courage. I am convinced that my recent shift in thinking about my own ability to take risks, speak up, shape my culture, and influence future generations is due to the stories of biblical women inspiring me and paving the way for my brave moments. I owe so much to them. I failed so many times by hiding behind a false identity and being a different person in the dark than I was in the light.

Their lives have taught me that it's my character—not my context—that defines my choices.

I have been shaped by their obedience, compelled to step into areas of ministry that I would never have dreamed would be possible for me. I witness the power of God in their lives. I am empowered to freely and fully embrace my place, path, and purpose because of the testimony of these powerful women's lives. Karoline M. Lewis writes:

> Unlocking your power as a woman in ministry means that you are able to verbalize how the Bible and your theology have made it possible for you to embrace your true self. That the biblical stories and the testimony you have heard from the pages of scripture have had a claim on your identity construction. That you know who you are not only because you know *whose* you

are, but because you have allowed that identity to shape deeply how you live and move in the world.[3]

My character is forged when I choose obedience to the Holy Spirit's prompting over fear of what "might" happen to me. My character is forged when I realize I'm on the wrong path and need to make amends for any emotional disturbance I've caused.

I've also realized the importance of my gender in shaping the way I read Scripture. The truth is that I, as a woman, will resonate with different aspects of the Bible than men will. I understand and recognize that there have not been enough women publicly interpreting the Bible to bring these resonances into any kind of balance with what is typically and traditionally heard in male interpretations.

Perhaps we haven't been as ready to marry the words "women" and "theology" in the same sentence. "Theology is a word we have associated with scholars, professors, pastors, and men, probably in that order."[4]

As a woman who studies and teaches the Bible, I know I have an obligation to give voice to interpretations that have either not been allowed or not been uttered aloud. In this moment, in this day, in this culture, there's so much empty space that waits to be filled with the beauty—including the messiness—of the feminine narrative. Lucy Peppiatt, in her book, *Rediscovering Scripture's Vision for Women*, writes:

> One of the ways of seeing alternative narratives in the Bible is either to tell the women's stories or to tell the stories from the point of view of the women. This is an invaluable exercise for both male and female preachers, and it is incumbent on all teachers of the Bible (preachers, theologians, Bible study leaders, youth workers, and children's workers) to focus as much on the stories of women as they do on the stories of the men. It is not just the girls and the women who need to hear the stories of women in the Bible. The boys and the men need to hear them too. They have mothers, grandmothers, sisters, daughters, wives, girlfriends, aunts, nieces, female friends, and colleagues. Hearing the story of how God includes women in his big story

will help women and men to see the women around them in a different light and open up possibilities in our imaginations for how women may be used by God in influential ways.[5]

There's much to say about the lives of the she-saints who were instrumental in partnering with God to move His story forward, culminating in Jesus' arrival on earth, despite the fact that they were women living imperfect lives. In fact, it was *because* they were imperfect women that I believe their stories were redeemed by God and written down to transcend cultures.

Where did bravery ever get me?

In the past, I clearly chose something the opposite of bravery more times than not. I have wrestled with using my voice to declare the *ezer kenegdo* image-bearing position of warrior-like strength[6] that God intended for women, beginning with Eve, especially when I realize that failing once does not mean no second chances.

I have wanted to self-silence the cry in me that has seen too much pain and suffering in the lives of women in my nation, and beyond, due to the fear of being labelled one of "those" feminists. I am for women. I am for men. I am for the Body of Christ coming together in a diverse unity, and the place of the best working out of that transpiring is within the local church.

My dear friend, Dr. Pam MacRae, a professor at Moody Bible Institute, wrote the following in a chapter she wrote, called "Finding Your Voice":

> If a woman internalizes the message asking her to limit her voice, and she self-silences, everyone is ultimately affected. It is dangerous for anyone to feel she is living on the periphery when engaging issues of theology and of knowing God. If a woman feels silenced, she is also likely to choose a posture of learned helplessness and dependence.[7]

In her book, *Half the Church*, Carolyn Custis James brings a threefold challenge to the church:

First, what message does the church offer women in the twenty-first century? The world needs a gospel vision of relationships between men and women. Will the Bible deliver?

Second, what will the church do to address the rampant suffering of women throughout our world? Will we join together in taking the lead in global advocacy… on behalf of the widow, the trafficked, the marginalized, and oppressed?

Third, what message are we sending to the world by how we value and mobilize our own daughters? Will the whole church openly benefit from women's gifts and contributions or will the body of Christ attempt to fulfill a mission that dwarfs our resources without the full participation of half the church? What is it costing us when half the church's gifts go untapped?[8]

This book is not about men's and women's roles; neither is this an academic work. Rather, it's a work of exploration. It's a book about the impact of women's bravery in biblical history on my life and one that I hope will influence your brave moments. This book is a rallying cry to all women to step into their brave moments—despite their context—because their "yes" matters.

Your "yes" matters.

I believe there are stunning stories of women, including yours, that need to be told and retold thousands of times from now until eternity. There's much space in God's story for our own stories to be brimming over. I need to be brave enough to tell my story, and you, yours. It matters.

I pray for you to lean into the lessons that come from studying the lives of biblical women, both past and present. I pray that you will begin to see yourself in at least one of their stories. I pray you will be shaped by the stories gifted to you by the inspired writers of Scripture so you might learn that *brave making* is directly tied to the *making of your character*.

As you look around, you'll begin to notice brave women choosing to say what needs to be said and to do what needs to be done when the moment comes.

You will know when it's time to *choose brave and make your bold move.* The Holy Spirit will prompt you. Be open to the moment when He says: "This is your *kairos*[9] moment. Step into it."

There's a cloud of female witnesses who forged the path for you through their example. You can step out with courage and clear the path for all those coming after you.

Don't conform. Don't be like everyone else. Be brave. Your bold moment awaits you.

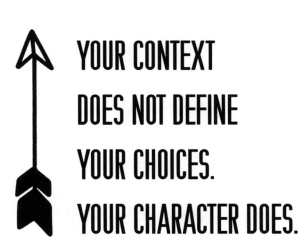

YOUR CONTEXT
DOES NOT DEFINE
YOUR CHOICES.
YOUR CHARACTER DOES.

PROLOGUE

What does it mean to be brave?

The definition of "brave" is to be ready to face and endure danger or pain, showing courage. "Brave" can also mean recklessly bold, extremely original, fearless, and daring.[10]

I believe that being brave means moving through fear to step into bold moments and, by doing so, influencing the trajectory of history and generations to come.

Bravery is an act of obedience because so often, we are cloaked in cowardice. We need to be tethered to someone braver than ourselves to move out in courage. It's the desire to obey a great God for a greater outcome that enables us to stand up, step out, and speak up when our knees are trembling. We know we could never do "the thing" or say "the thing" if God had not stamped His courageous character on our hearts.

If you don't believe that your brave will get you anything but more of a reputation as a troublemaker, or even being branded as a woman unwilling to submit to religious, political, social, or cultural norms, then you certainly shouldn't read any of the stories of the women we'll be looking at together. Don't do it! Put down this book immediately, and don't pick up your Bible again. It will wreck you, in all the best ways.

Where did the bravery of these women—past and present—get them? Why did they choose to look foolish and risk their reputations?

Their bravery forged the path on which you're now privileged to walk, even if you're experiencing a less-than-fairy-tale life. Their bravery got their stories included in the bestselling history book of all time; their stories are available on the New York Times Best Sellers' list, on Amazon, and wherever the Bible is sold. If their profiles were on Instagram today, their followers would be in the millions.

So where do *you* want your bravery to get you? Are you scared of doing something you've been thinking you should do for a very long time, and not doing that thing, just because you know can't control the outcome or how people will respond?

Perhaps your fears have as their source one or more of the following:

- low self-worth
- waiting painfully for something to change
- self-denial
- making sacrificial choices in crisis moments
- comparison
- wanting what you can't have
- not belonging
- moving forward with a shameful past
- speaking truth to power
- influencing generations

Good news: You're in great company! Throughout my life, I have struggled with *all* of the above limiting fears.

As a coach and leadership trainer, I have met and worked with hundreds of women who measure the goodness of God by how "safe" He allows their lives to stay. If He allows disruption, pain, suffering, or challenging circumstances, the natural response is to assume that either a) God is not really good, or b) He's not able to change their circumstance.

They have removed themselves from the biblical narrative or forgotten how relevant it is—particularly the significance of women strategically showing up in moments that are equally as challenging, and then managing in the midst of complexity to risk and believe in a future they couldn't see.

Depending on your family of origin and/or denominational background, you might have been taught to "keep your place" and regulate your voice to stay in the roles required by your family or your church. For many of you, this has not been an issue; you've found great joy serving in a sweet spot of ministry, marketplace, and/or family life.

But others of you have a heartbeat for using birthright gifts of leadership, teaching, preaching, visioning, and strategizing in the Body of Christ. Maybe you've found that the stories of brave women in the Bible have been sidelined to children's ministry classes, rather than shared from pulpit preaching. Who are your champions? Who is encouraging you? The importance of the biblical narrative of women and the character of God they represent is not mainstream in current gatherings of the church in which women represent *half of the body of Christ.*

If we are, indeed, half the church, should not the theology of our inherent value as image-bearers be woven more consistently into the fabric of the gospel's message?

Where did these amazing women fit in the historical timeline? God made covenants with well-known patriarchs. Hollywood has included in its cinematic portrayals Noah and the Ark, Moses and the Ten Commandments, Abraham and Isaac, and David and Goliath.

Yet interwoven in the middle of this covenantal timeline are the key women players, without whom the story of Jesus would never have come about. They were all, with their daunting bravery, instrumental in bringing about the redemption story as they worked in partnership with God's purposes. The truly brave ones chose to act in ways that no one around them was choosing. They chose to challenge the cultural and religious norms of the day and dared to be both determined and different.

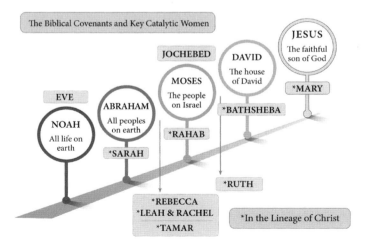

Where does bravery ever get you?

It gets you in the slipstream of the bigger story and makes you a heroine for generations to come.

These words are for *you*, friend. They're written for those of you paralyzed with debilitating fear. They're written for those of you who know your heart beats brave, just waiting to be championed into action. They're written for those of you who understand that when you don't step into your moment, it remains empty. You are the woman who doesn't want to miss being part of the adventure.

Your brave is for now. Your bold is for future generations. Choose courage. You have an opportunity to be a culture reformer, instead of allowing culture to continue to pressure you to conform to its norms.

Let's explore this epic tale together. I invite you to step into the very beginning with me and consider how God set this brave story into motion.

Are you with me?

 YOUR BRAVE IS
FOR NOW.
AND YOUR BOLD IS
FOR FUTURE GENERATIONS.

1. MAKING WAY FOR BRAVE

Don't Measure Brave
with a Faulty Measuring Stick

*The depth of darkness to which you can descend and still live is
an exact measure of the height to which you can aspire to reach.*
—Pliny the Elder[11]

I WAS STUCK AND COULDN'T MOVE.

It wasn't the first time I had been in this position. I lay there, on my bed, forcing the zipper on my jeans to move up just a little higher.

My high-school years were filled with trying to fit into jeans that were at least one size too small because I measured my value by my jean size. I was determined to avoid going up into the double digits! I should've been wearing a size twelve, but there I was, trying to squeeze myself into the size eight jeans that required me to lay flat on the bed to get the zipper up. I can't describe the acrobatics needed to get up and moving in those bad boys.

I've always been a measurer. How about you? If I gave you sixty seconds to write down all the things you measure in any given day, how many could you come up with?

You could probably write your list quickly, without even thinking. Your list would include measuring ingredients for the cupcakes you made that day, the time it took to carpool the kids back and forth to school and activities, how quickly your roots were growing in, steps walked on your Fitbit, how many dollars were left in the bank after the mortgage payment, how fast your church or ministry was growing, how many women registered for your conference, how many friends you could count on to be there in a crisis, how many years until the kids leave home.

Why did all of these things just flow from your head onto paper?

Measuring is second nature for most women. We're constantly making mental equations like a human calculator, unaware we're even doing it. The whirring of the measuring tape is constantly running. We measure our time, our trajectory, our "stuck-ness," our goodness, our badness, and ourselves, one measuring moment at a time.

We translate the sums of our calculations, the inches on the measuring tape, and the checklist of daily accomplishments into a value judgment about our worth. Most of the time we come up short.

"I should've walked more steps today."

"If I'd been a better mother and spent more time with my son, he wouldn't be making such bad choices."

"If I could fit into my size eight jeans, my husband would still pay attention to me."

"If I were a better leader and had more followers, God would increase my platform."

Our increases and decreases are directly tied to what we've measured and the narrative we've created. If we've measured how long God's taken to answer our prayers, then we assume He doesn't hear us or love us like we thought He did. If we're living with financial abundance, we measure God's blessing over us and create belief systems about others' worth. We take out our measuring sticks of comparison and come up with a score on how brave we are based on those who are either braver than us, or "cowards."

"She parachuted out of an airplane; she must be brave."

"She walked out of her marriage; she must be a coward."

We feel good or bad about our own bravery depending on to whom we choose to compare ourselves. It is, and always has been, a numbers game with us. And the numbers just aren't adding up.

An appropriate measurement of "just how brave is brave?" needs to start with the beginning of everything, with the Creator of everything. We need to start with the brave-making God of the universe. He's the only true measure.

Where did God's bravery ever get Him?

GOD MADE WAY FOR BRAVE

In Genesis 1:1, it says, "*in the beginning, God created the heavens and the earth*" (NIV).

The earth's beginning, for sure. Our beginning, absolutely. But *His* beginning?

We want to measure our beginning and end because we're human, and because measuring is second nature. God began earth and humanity in Genesis 1, but where did *God* begin? Could we even measure it if we knew?

As much as we'd love to measure God's beginning and end, we can't. So then we should ask, how *measurable* is God? How *brave* is God?

In his magnificent song exalting the victory of Yahweh over Pharaoh and the gods of Egypt, Moses cried, "*Who is like You among the gods, O Lord? Who is like You, majestic in holiness, awesome in praises, working wonders?*" (Exodus 15:11, NIV).

Dr. Kenneth R. Cooper tried to begin to answer the question "How immeasurable is God?" and has given us insight into the mystery of the answer:

> The question is at best rhetorical, since among all the gods of the earth in all the ages of time, there is NONE like the God of Moses. He is incomparable! There is no one He can be measured against. He is indescribable! There is no one he can be described in relationship to! He is incomprehensible! {That means we cannot measure someone we cannot comprehend}. However, in spite of our inability to comprehend God, He has revealed Himself in the pages of Scripture and in the Person of His Son.[12]

We can't wrap our heads around His immeasurability, so we think up diminishing images of Him. We try to contain Him as our "genie" and feed him with a prayer or two every now and then. We put Him on *our* schedule, in *our* world, at *our* beck and call, under *our* control. He exists for us. He's only as brave as we make Him. So it makes sense that He should be ready to solve all of our problems and fix the issues with the people and situations around us.

We measure God's bravery in direct relation to whether He's answering our prayers the way we feel He should.

But this isn't the God of the Bible—not even close. He was never meant to serve our whims. In the preface to *The Knowledge of the Holy*, A.W. Tozer calls this *"the loss of the concept of majesty."*[13] He explains this loss as a gradual diminishing of the concept of God as the concerns of the world and its culture encroach upon the church. With our loss of the sense of majesty, we also lose our awe and consciousness of His divine presence.[14]

I often wonder if this little seed of loss began with the first woman God created. Maybe she lost the wonderment of the wonderful Father who had fashioned her in His image. We are so like her, aren't we? (We'll get to Eve's story in the next chapter.)

Tozer also says, *"left to ourselves, we tend immediately to reduce God to manageable terms. We want to get Him where we can use Him, or at least know where He is when we need Him. We want a God we can in some measure control."*[15]

Read that last sentence again: "We want a God we can in some measure control."

We believe we can't just let God be God. We can't let Him be wild, amazing, creative, scary, fierce, and truthful, eyes blazing with fire, passion, and love for us. We can't do that because if we can't *measure* Him, then we can't *control* Him.

Are you trying to measure God? Are you trying to control Him for your purposes? He's out of the box, whether or not you "let Him out," because He was never in the box. You did not conceive of God; He conceived the thought of you before the earth and the land and the sea and the sky even existed.

How then can you now speak to Him and say, "I don't like my marriage! It doesn't measure up to what I thought You would make happen for me. Can't You do something?"

Or "God, I'm not happy with my church, my kids, my mother-in-law, my weight, my Netflix choices…" etc.

Or "God, could You be reduced to my little world of control and give me what I think I want?"

Maybe you and I need to be jolted back to the unchanging truth that since God is sovereign and rules over His creation, His majesty alone reveals Him to be a God we can't manage, measure, or manipulate.

And yet, in this beautiful space of immeasurability in which God alone exists, He so tenderly reveals to us His character.

First, God has a relationship with His people. Let's read the words of Isaiah 40:9–11:

O Zion, messenger of good news,
shout from the mountaintops!
Shout it louder, O Jerusalem.
Shout, and do not be afraid.
Tell the towns of Judah,
"Your God is coming!"
Yes, the Sovereign Lord is coming in power.
He will rule with a powerful arm.
See, he brings his reward with him as he comes.
He will feed his flock like a shepherd.
He will carry the lambs in his arms,
holding them close to his heart.
He will gently lead the mother sheep with their young. (NLT)

God is our Shepherd, carrying the lambs, carrying you, close to His heart. Is He reduced in this moment? No! Rather, He is even *more* magnificent in this moment because He *chooses* to be with you. In contrast to the Old Testament pagan gods who were territorial and far removed from the people who worshipped them, Yahweh identified the entire nation of Israel as His child, saying, *"Israel is my firstborn son,"* (Exodus 4:22, NIV).

The immeasurable God tends, gathers, and carries. He's brave enough to lower Himself down to swoop you up into His greatness and give you a place to belong. *"Who is like you, among the gods, O Lord?"* (Exodus 15:11, NLT). The answer is no one but God, the immeasurable God.

Second, God has infinite power.

In Isaiah 40:12–17, we read:

Who else has held the oceans in his hand?
Who has measured off the heavens with his fingers?
Who else knows the weight of the earth
or has weighed the mountains and hills on a scale?
Who is able to advise the Spirit of the Lord?
Who knows enough to give him advice or teach him?
Has the Lord ever needed anyone's advice?
Does he need instruction about what is good?
Did someone teach him what is right
or show him the path of justice?
No, for all the nations of the world
are but a drop in the bucket.
They are nothing more
than dust on the scales.
He picks up the whole earth
as though it were a grain of sand.
All the wood in Lebanon's forests
and all Lebanon's animals would not be enough
to make a burnt offering worthy of our God.
The nations of the world are worth nothing to him.
In his eyes they count for less than nothing—
mere emptiness and froth. (NLT)

When things get a bit "hairy" for us women—we run late, we fall, we fail, we get hurt, we hurt others, we are rejected, uninvited, unnoticed, and still rise another day to another load of laundry—I often wonder if all our questions about God could be reduced to two:

"Is He *able*?" and "Is He *good*?"

To believe in a God who is loving and compassionate, yet powerless to act on our behalf (good, but not able) would leave us with a feeling of utter helplessness. On the other hand, to believe that God's power and might were absolute but that he was unloving and unmoved by our hurts (able, but not good) would plunge us into despair.

Isaiah 40:9–11 tells us beyond the shadow of a doubt that He *does* care and He *is* able.

How is His infinite power shown?

GOD IS OMNIPOTENT

Isaiah reminds us that God is saying to us, "Just answer the question. Try your best. Here we go!

> *Who has measured the waters in the hollow of His hand,*
> *And marked off the heavens with a span [of the hand],*
> *And calculated the dust of the earth by the measure,*
> *And weighed the mountains in a balance*
> *And the hills in a pair of scales?*
>
> —Isaiah 40:12, AMP

Who is measuring, *what* is being measured, and *why*?

When Isaiah tells us that God "*measured the waters in the hollow of His hand,*" our questions might be, "which waters, how many waters, and just how big is the hollow of God's hand?"

We're challenged to imagine a God so vast that He measures all the waters of the earth in the hollow of *one* hand. How big is a hollow?

Cup your hand. You'll see that the hollow is the cuplike indention formed when your hand is partially closed. It's not the whole hand. How much water could you hold in the hollow of your hand when it's cupped? An ounce? Two?

When he mentioned "the waters," Isaiah meant *all* the waters in the world God had created. He measured and knew that all the waters, every drop, would fit into the hollow of His own hand.

Marva J. Dawn, in her book, *To Walk and Not Faint*, expresses the totality of water—all the seas, rivers, streams, lakes, ponds, oceans—more poetically. She notes:

> First, imagine all the raindrops in the world. Then add all the snowflakes and hailstones, the fog and the mists. Next, bring in all the creeks and ponds and puddles. Finally, add all the glaciers and snowpacks, the stream and rivers, the wells and

underground rivers and springs, and even all the lakes and the mammoth oceans. All the waters of the earth, added together— and God holds them in a single handful! Incredible![16]

God holds it all in the *hollow of one hand.*

In the next line of Isaiah 40:12, Yahweh marked off heavens with a span (of His hand). Hold up your hand and check the distance between the tip of the pinky and the tip of the thumb when your fingers are spread like a fan; it should be about nine inches. But how big is God's span?

It's big.

To Isaiah, the "heavens" likely referred to all the stars and black sky he could see at night from horizon to horizon, which is still a lot. Scientists have determined that the Milky Way Galaxy is 100,000 light-years in diameter, which is 100,000 times six trillion miles. And that's not even a fragment of the totality of the heavens.

God is not only powerful enough to have created everything, but also intelligent enough to have measured everything. That's why we must leave all the measuring up to Him.

I hope you are full of awe and wonder for this immeasurable God who carries, gathers, and tends to *you.*

GOD IS OMNISCIENT

Along with infinite power, God also holds infinite knowledge and wisdom (omniscience). Let's continue our reading:

> *Who has directed the Spirit of the Lord,*
> *Or has taught Him as His counselor?*
> *With whom did He consult and who enlightened Him?*
> *Who taught Him the path of justice and taught Him knowledge*
> *And informed Him of the way of understanding?*
> —Isaiah 40:13–14, AMP

If none but God can measure the heavens with a span, who can measure the Spirit of God. God Himself? Since God is greater than the heavens, greater than His own creation, how can any part of His creation even think of measuring Him?

GOD IS SOVEREIGN

In Isaiah 40:15–17, we read:

> *In fact, the nations are like a drop from a bucket,*
> *And are regarded as a speck of dust on the scales;*
> *Now look, He lifts up the islands like fine dust.*
> *And [the forests of] Lebanon cannot supply sufficient fuel to start a*
> *   fire,*
> *Nor are its wild beasts enough for a burnt offering [worthy of the*
> *   LORD].*
> *All the nations are as nothing before Him,*
> *They are regarded by Him as less than nothing and meaningless.*
> *   (AMP)*

Don't bother messing with Him because he has already taken measure of everything and everyone that was or ever will be, and they are dust, a speck.

GOD STANDS ALONE IN HIS UNIQUENESS

The words of Isaiah 40:18–20 tell us:

> *To whom then will you liken God?*
> *Or with what likeness will you compare Him?*
> *As for the cast image (idol), a metalworker casts it,*
> *A goldsmith overlays it with gold*
> *And a silversmith casts its silver chains.*
> *He who is too impoverished for such an offering [to give to his god]*
> *Chooses a tree that will not rot;*
> *He seeks out for himself a skillful craftsman*
> *To [carve and] set up an idol that will not totter. (AMP)*

Have you tried to compare God with someone, something? The truth is, you can't. God can't be measured. God is immeasurable. God is sovereign. God holds a unique place as the only One who ever was, is, and will be who cannot be measured—*ever*.

You can't measure your own brave unless you have a measure of your value. The faulty measuring of my bravery didn't just suddenly "kick in" when I reached womanhood. No, it was faulty from the moment I was born.

My mother had given birth to my oldest sister, Caroline, my brother Kenneth, and then Marianne. Marianne was two years old when it was my turn to enter this world. And then tragedy struck.

Marianne died of pneumonia while my mother was still pregnant with me. Struggling with guilt that she could've prevented it—even though it was absolutely untrue—my mother was depressed and grieving while carrying me. My birth circumstances affected me, as I was born feeling unwanted, unloved. There was so much sadness that had come before my arrival; I always had a sense I shouldn't have been born at all.

It doesn't make sense that my birth circumstances would be measured against the destiny I could have in the future. But I thought it did. I kept measuring myself against the voices that said, "You shouldn't have been born. You are not enough. You are taking up valuable space," and those "not-measuring-up" words followed me most of my childhood, teenage, and adult life.

I had to measure my worth and values, and for years, I defined myself by my *uns*. That is, I would tell you I was unwanted. Unfit. Unremarkable. Undefined. And *unbrave*. I was a coward. Cowards try to prove their worth. The brave ones never have to compare themselves to anyone in the first place.

I believe that many of you have stories that you have marked as "unbrave."

You might have thought that God was able to change your circumstances, past or present, but He just wasn't that good. Or you might have thought that He desired to change your circumstances, but just didn't have the power to.

My prayer for you, as you've now been reminded of God's loving, infinite, powerful character, is that you understand that He is both *able* and *good*.

Maybe He has allowed circumstances in your life because He's making you brave in the midst of the battle. But this is certain: You never need to question whether God made the way for you by being brave Himself.

What's the biggest risk you've ever taken? What did it cost you?

Maybe we can ask that question of God; maybe we *do* ask that question of God. When the stakes are high and everything and everyone is against us and our backs are up against a wall, we cry to God, "Wait a minute! Don't You see what I'm up against? I went out on a limb here, and now *this* is happening. And, by the way, when did *You* ever risk anything?"

He did. He took a huge risk when He put the man and woman He had lovingly created *in His garden* and gave them a choice whether to love Him back. And then He took the biggest risk of all when He allowed Himself, through His only Son, Jesus, to give His life so that we could keep ours. God fully knew that we would reject Him and crucify Him. He was brave anyway.

There is a danger here in even assuming that God could take a risk and lose. The mystery of God's identity is so unfathomable and the reason He will always be worthy of our worship. Was His risk calculated? Was He weighing the stakes of His commitment to His creation before He made the first declaration of life and light over the world? Or was God so overflowing with love that He recklessly chose to spend it on loving us—no matter what it cost Him?

I can't explain it. Even in the asking of the questions, I am brought to my knees in wonder at what makes God, *God*. I do know that He is Love, and every single one He chose to create and relentlessly pursue has a choice to turn to Him.

When bravery is mixed with love, it creates an opportunity for a new destiny to unfold.

Where did bravery ever get God?

It got Him right into the middle of our world, and He has chosen us to be in the middle of His. If we don't think God was ever brave enough because He hasn't answered our prayers, then we've been using a faulty ruler.

When nothing else would bridge the gap between His holiness and our unholy lives, He sent Himself.

What can be braver than that?

So don't measure God with a faulty measuring tool; He can't be measured because He's immeasurable.

He's only ever wanted to *be with us*. Imagine the God of the universe wanting to be with those He created. His first Garden was designed for Him to enjoy unbroken fellowship with Adam and Eve. Now that's risky—and *brave*.

And into this perfect, majestic world God had created for mankind entered Eve.

WHEN BRAVERY
IS MIXED WITH LOVE,
IT CREATES AN OPPORTUNITY
FOR A NEW
DESTINY TO UNFOLD.

2. A BRAVE COMEBACK-EVE

Don't Give Up After the First
(or Second) Failure

You are always free to choose...
but you are never free from the consequences of your choices.
—Anonymous

JENNIE'S STORY:

For me, being brave and taking action meant admitting I had a drug and alcohol problem and that addiction to these substances had taken over my life. I would leave my home every chance I could, leaving my husband so that I could pursue a lifestyle of partying, getting high, and being unfaithful. Eventually, I was caught in the lies I had told and my husband and I began the process for divorce because we saw no other way to "fix" things.

I was tempted to do what I always did in the past: Cut my losses, move, find a new relationship and new friends... but the fear that the cycle of addiction would repeat itself was not something I could ignore this time. I decided to be brave and admit the truth, that my life was out of control and I couldn't solve this problem on my own (if I could have, I would have already).

I began by taking small steps of admission to those closest to me. I began listening to what those closest observed of me and what they thought would be good next steps towards a healthy life. After doing this, I was finally ready to get professional help so that the cycle wouldn't repeat itself again in another couple of years.

Eight weeks later, I entered a twelve-month, live-in rehabilitation program called Teen Challenge. I had a lot of fear going into the program… fear [that] I would quit early and fear that this program wouldn't work. I feared [that] I couldn't change and I feared facing my past. I also feared that I would never be forgiven of my past once I admitted to it.

Each day took courage… courage to trust the process and courage to stay the course. By the grace of God, I discovered the love and forgiveness of Jesus Christ during my time in rehab. Jesus provided the courage I needed for each day. He radically changed the entire trajectory of my life. I graduated from the program and have lived in successful recovery ever since.

I am thankful that by taking those brave steps towards surrender that God never let me down. I am thankful that my husband also encountered Jesus during that time and we never did get that divorce. We are still married today and have been blessed with two beautiful children.[17]

Have you ever made choices that "seemed like a good idea at the time?" We should never be surprised when we give in to the temptation to make wrong choices. After all, we're human. We bear the consequences of these choices, often for the rest of our lives. The deep pain lies in when the cycle of addiction, lying, escapism, and/or pretending we're someone we're not keeps repeating itself.

Eve was created out of Adam's rib. And she was *very, very* good. God was pleased with His handiwork; Adam was infatuated with her. God fashioned every fibre of her, every cell, every freckle, every curve, and said, "This is good!"

Eve was given three birthright gifts:

- Breath
- Beauty
- Belonging

From Eve's first breath, she didn't have to deal with family-of-origin issues, or a mother-in-law's expectations. She was literally created into a perfect environment. There was no one like her, no long line of women after whom to model herself. There was no mom's group, wife's group, entrepreneur's group, or a place to go for facials or manicures. She was sufficient in every way, and in complete compatibility with her husband and her Maker.

She was so beautiful that she could be naked without apology or even a second thought. That is the kind of beauty many of us wish we'd been born with. Eve had it. She was faultless, flawless, unblemished, unequalled, beyond compare, and sublimely suited to her perfect environment.

And she *belonged*. There was no form she had to fill out or a dating season with Adam to prove her love. She was welcomed without question into an immediate relationship with Adam and God. She belonged. And with that belonging, she was given a position that was *ezer kenegdo*—an equal match with her man.

The Hebrew word *ezer* has two original meanings, depending on its pronunciation: *to rescue/to save*, and *to be strong*. The word *ezer* is used twenty-one times in the Old Testament, consistently within a military context. The *ezer* is a warrior, just like you are a warrior.

The Hebrew word *kenegdo* means *opposite as to him* or *corresponding as to him*. Man and woman were uniquely and equally created. Man and woman are neither better nor less than each other.

Within this definition, we can see Eve as someone who was brave. Warriors must be brave, right? So why do we remember Eve's legacy as *not* brave? After all, she gave in to the first temptation that came along. She could've stood up to the serpent and then called God into the conversation, but she didn't. She was a coward; she was weak.

She wanted the one thing she couldn't have. Sound familiar?

How did someone arrive perfectly formed in a perfect world with the perfect companion and unbroken communion with God, and finding herself wanting the one thing she couldn't have?

It's a sickness as old as time itself, one pervasive in our current culture. Do you ever look outside what God has placed around you for your protection, and desire what you know will not be good for you? Do you *want* it just because you don't *have* it?

Even with all the love and beauty in the world, Eve still had an overwhelming desire to grasp something beyond that because she couldn't fully grasp God's immeasurable love for her. She measured her worth by the one poison she couldn't have. She had to say "yes" to that thing—that apple, that poison—because even in that perfect environment, a sinister voice inside her told her she was not enough just as she was. She had been safe, protected, loved, and cherished—yet oblivious of her susceptibility to be tempted.

Sometimes, when we don't know our own limits, we must trust God to set them for us so we don't find ourselves in deep trouble. God knows we can only control what we know; what we don't know can control us.

That "other voice"—the voice of the enemy—became louder than the voice of God in that moment of temptation, and drew Eve into places in herself she never knew existed. I'm not sure she even knew what she was capable of until she reached out, took and bit the fruit, and tried to spread the sickness by sharing the blame with Adam.

Here's the narrative from Genesis 3:3–7:

> *Now the serpent was more crafty than any of the wild animals the Lord God had made. He said to the woman, "Did God really say, 'You must not eat from any tree in the garden'?"*
>
> *The woman said to the serpent, "We may eat fruit from the trees in the garden, but God did say, 'You must not eat fruit from the tree that is in the middle of the garden, and you must not touch it, or you will die.'"*
>
> *"You will not certainly die," the serpent said to the woman. "For God knows that when you eat from it your eyes will be opened, and you will be like God, knowing good and evil."*
>
> *When the woman saw that the fruit of the tree was good for food and pleasing to the eye, and also desirable for gaining wisdom, she took some and ate it. She also gave some to her husband, who was with her, and he ate it. Then the eyes of both of them were opened, and they realized they were naked; so they sewed fig leaves together and made coverings for themselves.* (NIV)

I call this Eve's *old story*. Even in the short time she was living and walking on earth, her perfect new beginning quickly became old news as it was forced to an abrupt end. Sin as a result of disobedience could not be tolerated by a holy God in a perfect environment.

Three things happened in Eve's old story.

In her old story, Eve was distracted by discontent. Psalm 41 reminds us that when we're aware of what danger might be lurking, we can ask God to help us not be drawn towards evil or take part in wicked deeds. Had Eve cried out in that moment for God to come to her aid, could the story have turned out differently?

> *I call to you, Lord, come quickly to me; hear me when I call to you.*
>
> *May my prayer be set before you like incense; may the lifting up of my hands be like the evening sacrifice.*
>
> *Set a guard over my mouth, Lord; keep watch over the door of my lips.*
>
> *Do not let my heart be drawn to what is evil so that I take part in wicked deeds along with those who are evildoers; do not let me eat their delicacies.*
>
> *But my eyes are fixed on you, Sovereign Lord; in you I take refuge—do not give me over to death.*
>
> *Keep me safe from the traps set by evildoers, from the snares they have laid for me.*
>
> *Let the wicked fall into their own nets, while I pass by in safety.*
>
> (NIV)

Eve was created with free will; this opened the door to the possibility that at some point, she would be faced with a significant choice. Did she honestly believe she was choosing between *good* and *better*, or was there a slight awareness that the tree of the knowledge of good and evil would result in more *evil* than *good*? How much did Eve know?

Had she been fully content, she wouldn't have listened to the serpent. One moment, she had everything anyone could ever want. In the next moment, she lost it all.

Do *you* have seeds of discontent in your life? Here are some questions you can ask yourself:

- In which ways do I identify with Eve in *my* old story?
- What's the biggest reason for discontentment in my life? What am I hoping for that I don't have?
- Has discontentment robbed me of joy? If so, how?
- What's the antidote to discontentment for me?

In her old story, Eve was deceived by dishonesty. The serpent outright lied to Eve when he told her, "you will not certainly die." Eve was deceived. The enemy's voice must have been convincing and believable, but because it was a lie, it stood in direct opposition to God's truth.

Here are some questions to consider as you think about the lies you believe about yourself, your life, and God.

- What's the biggest lie consuming me right now?
- Where did it come from?
- What truth can replace the lie?
- Do I believe God's love is for everyone else, but that I somehow am *not* worthy of it?
- What will it take for me to say, "no more!" to that lie?

In her old story, Eve was discouraged by defeat. Ask yourself the following questions as you dig down a bit to see what discouragement might be sitting in your soul:

- Is there a setback I can't get past and for which I believe God will never be able to forgive me?
- Do I continually experience defeat in the same area (lack of faith, jealousy, anxiety, anger, etc.)?
- What can I do to have victory over this area and move forward?
- What's my biggest "I'm not…" that I struggle with? What's the "I am…" I'll replace it with?

Where did Eve's bravery get her?

How can we even answer this when we have seen Eve be *anything but* brave?

I believe Eve's bravery was being forged through this defining moment of disobedience, as she carried the weight of her action's consequences into her future. I believe that the shame she felt when she realized she was naked, her need to run from God, and the broken trust with both Adam and God had her doing some serious soul-searching. Perhaps in those moments, hiding from God, she asked herself, "Is this the woman I want to be? Can I ever recover from this huge failure?"

I believe that God, full of grief that the man and woman He had created for fellowship had betrayed His trust, was fully prepared to give Eve a second chance.

Who says "no" to second chances? Had God been unkind in His grace, perhaps Eve would've continued her obedience in ways we can't even imagine. Instead, God cursed the serpent and sent Adam and Eve packing, banished from the garden, bearing the burden of working for their living on a hard earth, with pain in childbearing—*but* with the gift of His presence. He joined them in their new life, and has desired to be present in *our* lives ever since.

What happened when Eve had to leave the garden and start her new life? What did bravery look like for her?

BRAVERY IN A MARRIAGE IN WHICH YOUR TRUST IS BROKEN

Can you imagine the second Eve took the bite of fruit, then Adam took the bite, and they were face-to-face with their sin and with each other? What does a raw moment of regret do to a marriage?

> *She also gave some to her husband, who was with her, and he ate it. Then the eyes of both of them were opened, and they realized they were naked; so they sewed fig leaves together and made coverings for themselves.*
>
> —Genesis 3:6–7, NIV

Adam was standing right there! He could have talked her out of it, called God into the crisis, or told the serpent to take a hike. But he was a silent accomplice to the first disobedient act of mankind. We know their relationship was broken when Adam tried to blame Eve.

> *The man said, "The woman you put here with me—she gave me some fruit from the tree, and I ate it. Then the Lord God said to the woman, "What is this you have done?" The woman said, "The serpent deceived me, and I ate."*
>
> —Genesis 3:12–13, NIV

I'm sure Eve would have loved to double-back on Adam and remind him that he was with her when the deed was done. Instead, she pinned it on the serpent and didn't own up to the responsibility of her action. I can't imagine this married couple had much to say to each other while they were hiding from God, lying to Him, and then having a "sewing session" to cover up their nakedness with fig leaves. The tension between them resulting from the shame-and-blame game must have been intense.

How does a marriage recover from such betrayal? I believe it took all the bravery Eve could muster to keep on going and stay with the man who had betrayed her to her Father. What other options did she have? We know she left the garden with Adam and stayed with him until death. I'm not sure if their relationship was ever fully restored.

Have you ever felt the same as Eve in your marriage or another significant relationship with someone whom you trusted when you were betrayed? How do you keep on trusting when you're just as responsible for creating the situation in which the betrayal took place, and *especially* when you're innocent? We can learn from Eve that, despite the fact that things were shaky between her and Adam, Adam named her the "mother of all living things."

Perhaps there was a seed of hope there for Eve that she could still fulfill the purpose for which God had created her. Would she and Adam be drawn to each other again in order to produce a generation? Yes!

BRAVERY AS A MOTHER WHEN YOUR CHILDREN ARE BROKEN

Adam made love to Eve, who later gave birth to Cain, which Eve acknowledged was the Lord's doing. *"With the help of the Lord I have brought forth a man"* (Genesis 4:1, NIV).

Unfortunately, with Abel's birth, the narrative turned ugly again as the sin of jealousy crept in and the first murder on earth took place. How do you recover from one of your children murdering the other? Did Eve ask herself, "What kind of mother am I?" Did she feel responsible?

Eve was dealing with a marriage that was perhaps healing slowly, and then the pain of losing a child in such a horrendous act, and then living with the remaining murderous child. The brokenness in this family must have been profound. It's one thing to fail yourself, but to witness your own children committing such an evil act would be almost too much to bear.

Eve showed her bravery in this season, because she lived to mother another child, and another. When her fourth son, Seth, was born, she acknowledged God again, saying, *"God has granted me another child in place of Abel, since Cain killed him,"* (Genesis 4:25, NIV).

EVE'S DESTINY IN HER NEW LIFE

I believe Eve honestly felt she had been given more than one second chance. I believe she had the courage to keep on going even though she experienced failure, not once, but twice, and with consequences that changed the course of all of our histories.

I believe that Eve—the mother of all living things—became a woman of bravery and influence. After the birth of Seth, "… *people began to call on the name of the Lord"* (Genesis 4:26, NIV).

Was it Eve's faith in and gratitude towards God that influenced the next generations to remember God and call on Him for themselves? She could have easily become bitter and despondent, as her life had carried so much loss thus far. But she kept going, walking out her destiny to not only be part of *creating*, but influencing, future generations with her testimony of God's grace and forgiveness in her life.

I attended a conference of female clergy ("Lydia's Daughters") on September 17, 2019 (Oakville, Ontario), and a young woman named Taryn Ferrede delivered a powerful five-minute poetic speak that had everyone in the room mesmerized by the beauty of the story of God she shared from a woman's perspective.

Her words—"Eve will forever pay the price for Adam's silence with her own"—left me stunned.

I wonder how deeply Adam's silence in the moment when eternal life and earthly death hung in the balance left its ugly mark on Eve's heart. I wonder how she had to carry the knowledge that her words would never hold as much value or credibility as his, because she was a woman. I wonder how much we, as women, have been diminished in speaking our wild and brave words because we feel they don't carry as much weight as a man's?

Carrying the betrayal because of Adam's silent agreement to devastating sin in the moment, with consequences that reach into my world, could have kept any woman down. But she kept going, worshipped God, and through her pain, sowed seeds of faith into the next generations.

Where did Eve's bravery get her?

To you and your life, right now. You are I are linked to Eve and her choices. We often focus on what we can't have, we experience betrayal in our closest relationships, and we know what it's like to have children who make poor choices. Our story is linked to Eve's because even when it seems we're out of options, our bravery and our obedience to God's promptings, will keep us in the game, despite our first (or second) failure, and keep us moving forward.

Our worst choice on our worst day can never disqualify us from God's love. And neither will the choices our spouses, our children, or others close to us make.

When you are overwhelmed with tasks, choices, and life, read and take to heart the following prayer from Ted Loder as an encouragement to not exclude God from those pivotal moments. I believe that, had Eve called upon God when faced with the lying voice of the enemy in her ear, we would still be enjoying life in the garden.

Holy One,
there is something I wanted to tell you,
but there have been errands to run,
bills to pay,
arrangements to make,
meetings to attend,
friends to entertain,
washing to do...
and I forget what it is I wanted to say to you,
and mostly I forget what I'm about or why.
O God,
don't forget me, please,
for the sake of Jesus Christ...
O Father in Heaven,
perhaps you've already heard what I wanted to tell you,
What I wanted to ask is,
forgive me,
heal me,
increase my courage, please.
Renew in me a little of love and faith,
and a sense of confidence,
and a vision of what it might mean
to live as though you were real,
and I mattered.
What I wanted to ask in my blundering way is
don't give up on me, don't become too sad about me,
but laugh with me,
and try again with me,
and I will with you, too.[18]

Like Eve, you have a new story. Remember God's words: *"I have loved you with an everlasting love; I have drawn you with unfailing kindness"* (Jeremiah 31:3, NIV).

There's nothing you can do to cause God to stop loving you or take your destiny out of your reach. Eve did not have her name, or her destiny, taken from her.

God is bigger than your first mistake, or your second or third. He didn't abandon Eve; He will never abandon you. He is present to help you break your bad choices and replace them with a worshipper's heart.

Reflect on the following verses for a few minutes, and see if the truth of all that is still possible in your life because of God's love encourages your heart:

> *For I am convinced that neither death nor life, neither angels nor demons, neither the present nor the future, nor any powers, neither height nor depth, nor anything else in all creation, will be able to separate us from the love of God that is in Christ Jesus our Lord.*
> —Romans 8:38–39, NIV

Eve was the woman with the greatest comeback after the greatest failures in her life, and you can be too. Eve's worst choice on her worst day could not separate her from God's love.

THE BRAVE TRUTH

- Don't measure your value by what you don't or can't have. Measure your value by the One who owns it all.
- God is your best hope in breaking your bad choices. It's always His desire to bring you to your destiny.
- Remember that you worship a God who is immeasurable and loves you, failure after failure, with the best love you could ever be loved with.

How do you measure your brave after you have failed? Just how brave did Eve have to be? What does it take to bounce back after your worst choice on your worst day? *Bravery.* Your bravery to get up and keep moving just one more day will take you one step closer to your future. God goes with you. And I am your biggest champion.

STUDY QUESTIONS

1. How do you resonate with Eve's story? What do you measure? How does that line up with what God measures?
2. What was your worst choice on your worst day? What's your biggest regret? Have you ever thought this regret disqualified you from God's best for you?
3. Do a quick count. From Genesis 1:1 through Genesis 2:25, how many times does the word "good" appear in the creation story? Who says it? When? Why?
4. Read Genesis 3. How many times do you see the word "good" mentioned? Why do you think that is?
5. Read Genesis 4:1 and 4:25–26. What comes through in Eve's words?
6. Do you think Eve should have been granted a second chance to break her "bad?"
7. Do you believe you deserve a second chance to break *your* bad?

A MAKING BRAVE PRAYER

Dear God:
Please untie the knots
that are in my mind, my heart and my life.
Remove the have nots, the can nots and the do nots that I have in my mind.
Erase the will nots, may nots,
might nots that may find a home in my heart.
Release me from the could nots, would nots and should nots that obstruct my life.
And most of all, Dear God,
I ask that you remove from my mind, my heart and my life all of the 'am nots'
that I have allowed to hold me back, especially the thought
that I am not good enough. Amen. (Anonymous)

EVERY TIME YOU CHOOSE
TO GIVE UP CONTROL,
YOU BECOME STRONGER,
BOTH IN THE WAITING,
AND IN THE LETTING GO.

3. A BRAVE WAITING—SARAH

Don't Focus on
Things You Can't Control

You are brave, even in the most subtle ways, and you may not always feel like the fire that you are, but you will shine on anyway.
—Morgan Harper Nichols[19]

WHEN WE LAST HEAR OF EVE (GENESIS 4:26), SHE AND ADAM HAD LEFT the garden; their descendants were calling on the name of the Lord and worshipping Him. What followed in Genesis was a story of those descendants, generation after generation, turning from God until they became part of a world gone wrong.

God called Noah as the only righteous and blameless man living on the earth to build an ark. God sent the flood, and when the land eventually dried up, mankind could have a new beginning. But mankind decided they needed to control God, so they built the Tower of Babel. God then had to confuse their language and scatter them all over the world as a consequence of their pride. At last, we encounter Abram and Sarai. In Genesis 12:1–3, we read:

The Lord had said to Abram, "Go from your country, your people and your father's household to the land I will show you. I will make you into a great nation, and I will bless you; I will make your name great, and you will be a blessing. I will bless those who bless you, and whoever curses you I will curse; and all peoples on earth will be blessed through you." (NIV)

Who received this first promise? Not Sarai, but Abram. *Hmm, I think this kind of promise takes two,* she might have thought when Abram relayed the promise to her.

During the next while, much happened; there was a famine, and then Lot, Abram's nephew, left for Sodom and Gomorrah. Eventually, the city in which Lot chose to settle down with his family became so corrupt that Abram had to pray to God to rescue him.

Then Abram received a second promise, a covenant between him and God that could never be broken.

God was changing the context in which His promise was to be fulfilled. It was a calling for Abram to move into something new, a new paradigm, a new environment. This "big-sky" thinking required Abram to understand that he was holy, set apart for God's purposes.

On the way to the new land, Abram defaulted on his integrity. He dishonoured Sarai by letting the Egyptian Pharaoh believe she was his sister and allowing her to become another man's possession. He and Sarai could have already had a lack of trust deeply embedded in their relationship.

> *After this, the word of the Lord came to Abram in a vision:*
>
> *"Do not be afraid, Abram. I am your shield, your very great reward."*
>
> *But Abram said, "Sovereign Lord, what can you give me since I remain childless and the one who will inherit[c] my estate is Eliezer of Damascus?" And Abram said, "You have given me no children; so a servant in my household will be my heir."*
>
> *Then the word of the Lord came to him: "This man will not be your heir, but a son who is your own flesh and blood will be your heir." He took him outside and said, "Look up at the sky and count the stars—if indeed you can count them." Then he said to him, "So shall your offspring be."*
>
> *Abram believed the Lord, and he credited it to him as righteousness.*
>
> —Genesis 15:1–6, NIV

Who else would be necessary to fulfill this promise? It would require a woman's womb.

This is where we first read of Sarai's reaction to the promise given to Abram, not her. She was suspicious, most likely already of Abram, and perhaps of the God who had made such a big promise to him.

She knew it would take a woman for the promise to be fulfilled, so she decided to take matters into her own hands. She determined to get things moving. After all, she was getting older, and time was running out. Sarai had something to prove.

> *Now Sarai, Abram's wife, had borne him no children. But she had an Egyptian slave named Hagar; so she said to Abram, "The Lord has kept me from having children. Go, sleep with my slave; perhaps I can build a family through her." Abram agreed to what Sarai said.*
> —Genesis 16:1–2, NIV

Sometimes getting involved in the situation to move things forward can be seen as a courageous act. In Sarai's case, the opposite was true. Her solution—to send her slave to her husband—was an act of cowardice and unbelief. She couldn't believe that God would be good enough, able enough to grant her a son.

Sarai's two questions were the same as Eve's: Is God *able*? Is God *good*? Perhaps she believed the first, or the second—or neither. If Abram couldn't be trusted, could God? Without a belief in God's ability and goodness, Sarah couldn't wait it out. It was time to act.

Sarai was hiding in the shadows as God's promise—which required her participation for fulfillment—came to Abram. Yet she did not step up to claim her role in the story. She was still receiving the promise through someone else, not God directly.

Sarai had no idea she was called to a starring role in the bigger story. This wasn't just about Abram. Sarai had no idea she was going to be given a new name in the bigger story. She was used to wearing her identity as a used, barren woman.

Sarai had no idea she was going to be called the "mother of many nations" in the bigger story. She wasn't the one God made the covenant with, after all.

Sarai (later named Sarah) measured her value by the one thing she couldn't control: her barrenness. She chose to breach God's promise, creating an irreversible backlash.

This diagram helps us see the consequence of her inability to wait on God's timing, and how God stepped in at every moment to carry out His original plan.

THE BACKLASH OF SARAH'S BREACHING	THE BEARING OUT OF GOD'S BIDING
Sarai's brutal response She sends Hagar in to sleep with Abram and they have a child, Ishmael. It is not a happy home. Sarai is jealous of Hagar, and Hagar goads Sarai. There is much conflict. Eventually, when Isaac is borne to Sarah, who now has a new name, Abraham sends Hagar and Ishmael away. Hagar is in despair and feels alone and abandoned.	*God's bearing out* God sees Hagar and protects her and Ishmael as long as his descendants were alive.
The broken line of lineage The covenantal promise was to come through the child Abraham and Sarah had together, not through Abraham and Hagar's union.	*God's best plan* Hagar and Abraham's union produces Ishmael's line, from which comes the Muslim race. From this line there is no covenantal relationship with the God of Israel.
A boomerang of blame There was blame between Sarah and Abraham, Abraham and Hagar, and Hagar and Sarah. It was a triangle of blame. Sarah had pre-empted the promise of God. Perhaps because the promise had not come to her directly, she had a hard time believing it.	*A blessing on Sarah's Life* In Genesis 17:15 we read: *"I will bless her richly, and she will become the mother of many nations. Kings of nations will be among her descendants."* God directs the promise to Sarah personally to refocus Sarah on his beautiful beyond and not her boomerang of blame.

"Sarai, if only you had *waited*!" we might cry out as we read her story.

Do you ever get caught up in measuring God's inability to meet your timeline? When things don't work out as you planned, do you, like Sarai, take matters into your own hands? There are consequences. And then you need to find someone to blame.

> SARAH'S BREACHING CREATED A BOOMERANG OF BLAME. GOD'S BIDING CREATED A BEAUTIFUL BEYOND.

Whom do you blame for having to wait? What have you done to come up with the solution yourself because you got tired of waiting on God?

But there's no brave making when you're busy manipulating God's promises.

In Genesis 17:2, God made clear His specific covenant with Abram: "*I will make you the father of a multitude of nations*" (NLT). He changed his name to Abraham, giving him belonging and purpose.

It's not until Genesis 17:15–16 that Sarai, whose name had been changed to Sarah, was directly mentioned in the promise:

> *Then God said to Abraham, "Regarding Sarai, your wife—her name will no longer be Sarai. From now on her name will be Sarah. And I will bless her and give you a son from her! Yes, I will bless her richly, and she will become the mother of many nations. Kings of nations will be among her descendants."* (NLT)

This was becoming personal for Sarah, yet she wasn't part of the conversation. She was hiding.

In Genesis 18:9–10, the three visitors returned:

> *"Where is Sarah, your wife?" the visitors asked. "She's inside the tent," Abraham replied. Then one of them said, "I will return to you about this time next year, and your wife, Sarah, will have a son!" Sarah was listening to this conversation from the tent.* (NLT)

She was listening *from the tent*—and she *laughed*. Before you judge, think about it: Wouldn't you? She wasn't about to trust Abraham or God with the most humanly impossible miracle of giving birth at her age. She was ninety. She couldn't accept that God had a plan for her.

I believe God was looking at Abraham but clearly speaking to Sarah. But she was hiding in the dark, too afraid to receive the promise meant for her, face-to-face. I wonder what would've happened if she had, instead, stepped out of the shadows into the light, looking into the eyes of God and receiving the promise. Her laughter wouldn't have been cynical or bitter, but rather joyful and hopeful.

You need to wrestle with whether you believe in God's ability and His goodness to fulfill His promises to you. Face Him. Challenge Him. Ask Him your hard questions. Let Him remind you of His promise. Staying where it's safe, in the tent, in the dark, casts shadows over the promise and leads to doubt. So come into the light. Choosing brave always happens in the light of the One who made a way for your brave.

What's happening while you are waiting? *God is at work.* Let's take another look at how God worked in Sarah's situation.

- He was redeeming the irreversible. He protected Hagar and still carries on the lineage He promised through Isaac—the lineage through which Christ would come.
- He was reuniting the irreconcilable. Abraham and Sarah united and she conceived.
- He was restoring the irreplaceable. God provided a lamb as a sacrifice for Isaac when Abraham was prepared to sacrifice him on the altar.

A few years ago, I was "stuck" in a transition in my life, struggling with bringing closure to the season and work I had finished in the arts. I felt stuck in a gap between where I had been and where I was going. I couldn't move forward and the waiting was killing me. I had always planned and strategized my way forward, but there was no plan or strategy in sight.

I was waiting for the next reason to get out of bed and have somewhere to go and people who needed what I could give them. I wondered whether God was done with me—whether He would ever call me into service again. I wondered if I had any use to God or His people. I felt old, used up.

Does that remind you of anyone?

I consulted a spiritual director to walk me through this time of waiting. I was seeking direction, action, and movement, but my coach was intentional about reminding me of the power of waiting. Sue Monk Kidd said, *"Waiting is the yeasting of the human soul."*[20]

Waiting is like making bread. Before you can taste its soft, chewy goodness, you have to mix it, knead it, and let it rise. It has to sit before it can be put into the warmth of the oven. The yeast needs to do its work.

And so I found myself waiting for the "yeast" to do its work so I would be ready for the next season of service. But it was taking a long time—*too* long, in my opinion.

"God's timing is not our timing." You've probably heard this expression. How do you honestly feel when people say this to you? Frustrated, I bet.

We know it's the truth, but it can make us angry that God isn't consulting with us before He reminds us that His time is not our time. We often have to wait in the dark until we see His powerful hand at work, but we wonder, "What are you waiting for, God? I've waited long enough."

Sometimes we think waiting is a noun—a *thing*, a static, unmoving burden. It sits on us heavily. We wait, we wait some more, with fear and dread that what we're waiting for is never going to happen because we've waited so long and it still hasn't happened. Then we lose hope and trust that anything will ever change.

The truth is that waiting is a verb—an active, exciting verb, full of energy, hope, and longing. There are two parts to it.

Part one is *bridling back*—to hold on to the reins; if you're racing too fast to get to the finish line, you'll run out of steam. Good jockeys know this when racing horses; they pace themselves. They have to bridle back the reins so they can make the sprint near the finish line.

The definition for this kind of waiting is to "stay where one is or delay action until a particular time or until something else happens."[21] It means to hold on, hold back, bide one's time, hang firm, stand by, sit back, and hold on to your horses. This kind of waiting is intentional. You don't want to get where you need to go too fast, because it's in the waiting that the race is won.

Part two of waiting is to *lean forward*—to lean into the future and anticipate that something amazing is going to happen. It means to be eagerly impatient—e.g., "I can't wait for tomorrow!" This kind of waiting means expectancy, to imagine and hope for, to look ahead for, to see coming, to grasp whatever is around the turn.

Why does God wait so long for His promises and purposes to be fulfilled?

In the waiting, God is both bridling back and leaning forward. He knows we shouldn't speed up the process because we'll run out of energy for the final sprint. At the same time, He's teaching us to lean forward in anticipation that we'll cross that finish line and finish well.

You see, Yahweh is a God who lives *kairos* moments, not *chronos* moments.

Why did God wait thousands of years to send Jesus?

Why did Jesus wait three days to rise from the dead?

Why is Jesus waiting so long before He comes again?

Why does God delay in anything?

We can create a basic timetable of God's major redemptive works in history, counting from the fall of Adam and Eve in the garden. In between each major event, there are larger periods of relatively uneventful history:

1. The fall of Adam and Eve
2. Wait two thousand years
3. The call of Abraham
4. Wait five hundred years
5. Giving the law to Moses at Mount Sinai
6. Wait fifteen hundred years
7. The ministry of Jesus
8. Wait two thousand-plus years
9. (in the future) Jesus' Second Coming
10. The New Heavens and the New Earth

God's plan of redemption seems to occur in small steps spread out over long lengths of time.

Maybe you think the following would've been a preferred order of events:

1. The fall of Adam and Eve
2. Wait twenty minutes
3. The death and resurrection of Jesus
4. Eternal bliss

The second order of events certainly would've saved a lot of horrible grief, bloodshed, death, sorrow, and sadness. There would be no wars, famines, or diseases. Adam and Eve would've made their sinful choice, Jesus would've immediately shown up to fix it… done.

But God deliberately delayed His redemptive plan. Why did He wait so long?

It's complicated. Compare it to raising a child. When is your child "ready" for kindergarten, or university? So much is going on in their development. The timeline is different for every child.

In God's world, we aren't aware of all of the moving pieces. It's complicated. Each decision affects someone else's.

I once heard pastor, author, and filmmaker Erwin McManus tell the story of trying to get to Edmonton, Canada, in January to speak at a major Christian conference. (It's extremely cold in Edmonton in January, so you must want or need to go there then!) Erwin kept experiencing flight delays and missed the conference, but then ended up on a different plane beside a man with whom he was able to converse and lead to Jesus. This conversation was ordained for Erwin, and he waited for planes that never came in order to get on the one plane and one seat God had saved for him. *"But do not forget this one thing, dear friends: With the Lord a day is like a thousand years, and a thousand years are like a day"* (2 Peter 3:8, NIV).

Kairos, as mentioned, is an ancient Greek word that refers to "the right or opportune moment." The ancient Greeks had two words to describe time: *chronos* and *kairos.* While *chronos* refers to chronological (or sequential) time, *kairos* refers to a period or season in which an event of significance occurs. While *chronos* is quantitative, *kairos* has a qualitative, permanent nature.

Kairos moments are the precise moments when heaven and earth collide. It's like the moment when an arrow is fired and meets its target.

Kairos moments can't be measured by speed or by distance, unlike *chronos* moments, which are.

We read of a *kairos* moment in Mark 1:15: "'*The time has come,' he said. 'The kingdom of God has come near. Repent and believe the good news!*'" (NIV).

In speaking of measurable, *chronos* time, Paul wrote in Acts 27:9, "*Much time had been lost, and sailing had already become dangerous because by now it was after the Day of Atonement*" (NIV).

In John 7:6, Jesus uses *kairos* in relationship to His time and *chronos* in relationship to his followers' human time: "*Therefore, Jesus told them, 'My time is not yet here; for you any time will do'*" (NIV).

We're known to want to use *chronos* time to measure God's *kairos* time. We want to measure the *kairos* moments of our lives with our measuring tape, rulers, and watches, and we realize it can't be done. We don't understand it.

It's like trying to convert inches into centimetres and miles into kilometres and none of it makes sense (unless you live in Canada!). The brightest minds have figured out how to convert these systems of measurement for our human understanding. But there's no measuring system to "convert" from *chronos* to *kairos* time.

Think about when you've wanted to control God in His gorgeous *kairos* moments of indeterminate, indefinite, mysterious time and reduce him to your *chronos* moments.

God decided to build a bridge of understanding from your *chronos* to His *kairos* so you could have a glimpse of His fluid yet always-on-time existence. The bridge was Himself, through His Son Jesus.

"Instead, he gave up his divine privileges; he took the humble position of a slave and was born as a human being. When he appeared in human" (Philippians 2:7, NLT).

Yahweh is a God who bides His time while He's busy building your future. He is bridling back in the saddle and helping you *not* to get there too fast because you're not ready. As much as what waits across that finish line is being prepared for you, you need to be prepared, built up, muscled up, shored up. You're being prepared for that glorious finish. There's a victory lap waiting for you, so you better be ready! You're going to need every second, every minute, and every additional lap around the track to be ready for what comes next.

Remember, while you're waiting, bridling back, and leaning in, God's at work. He's redeeming the irreversible.

Have you ever made decisions you wish in an instant you could do over?

My grandmother was moving from a small town in Manitoba to live with our family in Edmonton. Their vehicle met head-on with a car full of teenagers who were driving under the influence. She was killed instantly; the teenagers were fine. I often wonder if any of them had a moment when they wished they could reverse the moment of impact and made different choices *before* they got in the car.

God reversed the pain of my own birth experience and the rejection I felt. He has redeemed my story, which is being used to help others with their feelings of rejection.

He is *good* and He is *able*.

HE IS REUNITING THE IRRECONCILABLE

Colossians 1:19–20 reminds us that "... *in him all the fullness of God was pleased to dwell, and through him to reconcile to himself all things, whether on earth or in heaven, making peace by the blood of his cross*" (ESV).

He wants to reunite every wanderer back to Eden—to the garden described in Revelation, where we will live with Him forever. This takes *time*. We're often unaware of the work He completes and the promises He fulfills every day. He never sleeps. We're so focused on what He is (or isn't) doing on our behalf and on *our timeline* that we lose sight of all those who need to be reconciled back to Him before we're called to His presence forever.

HE IS RESTORING THE IRREPLACEABLE

Eve lost her home, but God gave her a new one. She lost a son, but He gave her a new one. He'll replace every tear you've ever cried out of loss and grief with joy and gladness. That's His promise to you. "*He will wipe every tear from their eyes, and there will be no more death or sorrow or crying or pain. All these things are gone forever*" (Revelation 21:4, NLT).

Eve's story flows right into Sarah's. She experienced firsthand the biding of God's time to bring her to her future, even while she breached the promise given to her and had to suffer the consequences of that decision.

THE BRAVE TRUTH

You see, at just the right time, when we were still powerless, Christ died for the ungodly.

—Romans 5:6, NIV

But when the set time had fully come, God sent his Son, born of a woman, born under the law, to redeem those under the law.

—Galatians 4:4, NIV

How do these verses remind us of the *kairos* moments that God moves in? You can count on these measures of truth and stake your life on them:

- God's purpose will not be thwarted by any promise you breach.
- God is your best bet in biding and bearing out. He always comes out the champion.
- You worship a God who fulfills all His promises to you in His own *kairos* time rather than your limited, finite, linear understanding of what you want Him to do in your *chronos* time.

How are you measuring God's *biding* in the *bearing out* His promise to you? Consider the following verses and measure it to your current level of patience with God's timing:

Trust in the Lord with all your heart, and do not lean on your own understanding. In all your ways acknowledge him, and he will make straight your paths.

—Proverbs 3:5–6, ESV

Sometimes we assume the brave thing to do is to act and to take matters into our own hands, like Sarah did. However, there are times when the brave thing to do is wait. And in the *kairos* moment promised to you, the promise is fulfilled—in His time for you.

Jesus could have come and healed Lazarus when he was still alive. Instead, He waited to raise him from the dead when he was already in his grave.

God could have made David king the day after he was anointed. Instead, He waited fifteen years to rise to the throne, many of those years spent fearing for his life, hiding out and running away from his own father-in-law.

God could have spoken to Moses in the desert about sending him to help free His people from slavery forty days after he ran away from Egypt. Instead, He made him wait for forty *years*.

We've looked at Sarah's own story of waiting; there are many other stories in the Bible to help us learn to bravely wait for our moment to arrive.

He tells us to wait for healing after we've been praying for years and there's no sign of recovery. He tells us to wait to fulfill His calling after He puts the passion in our hearts to serve Him. He tells us to wait to give us the desires of our hearts, whether it's a spouse, a baby, a new job, or an opportunity. He tells us to wait for direction when we're stuck at a dead end and we don't know where to go or what to do.

He could answer that same prayer you've been praying every night, for years, in a millisecond. The longer that prayer goes unanswered, the more it makes you question whether He even hears you.

Maybe by asking you to wait, He's making you brave—enough to build your faith during the valley in your life where it's too dark to see and too hard to believe. Brave enough to build your dependence on Him when you're barren and empty to see if He's truly all you desire and need. Brave enough to see how well you will trust and serve Him when you're still stuck in the background, doing seemingly nothing of significance. Brave enough to build your trust in Him when the storm keeps raging, the battle keeps going, and victory doesn't seem near. Brave enough to grow your faith and learn to depend only on Him. "We start squeezing the life out of our God-given influence when we attempt to take over and control."[22]

Don't focus on what you can't control. Bridle back. Lean forward. Breathe in the brave, no matter how long it takes you to see His promise to you fulfilled. God has something prepared for you. He asked some of the greatest women of faith to wait. He will come through in your *kairos* moment just like He came through for them.

Wait for it. It's coming.

STUDY QUESTIONS

1. How do you resonate with Sarah's story?
2. Describe a time when you stepped in prematurely to try to make something happen when your gut told you that you should wait? What were the results?
3. Have you ever made a decision you regretted and then experienced the boomerang effect of blame? Whom did you blame? Are you still blaming yourself?
4. Describe a time when you made a bad decision and God miraculously redeemed what seemed like irreversible results.
5. What are you waiting for right now? How long have you been waiting? How does it feel to wait?
6. Do you believe that God will provide "in the fullness of time" what He has promised you? What would that look like?
7. Are you able to step fully into God's *kairos* moments and surrender your *chronos* moments to His purposes for you?
8. Read through the following Scriptures for a reminder that waiting is a biblical principle that will help forge your character:

I believe that I shall look upon the goodness of the LORD in the land of the living! Wait for the LORD; be strong, and let your heart take courage; wait for the LORD!

—Psalms 27:13–14, ESV

Wait for the LORD and keep his way, and he will exalt you to inherit the land; you will look on when the wicked are cut off.

—Psalms 27:34, ESV

Therefore the LORD waits to be gracious to you, and therefore he exalts himself to show mercy to you. For the LORD is a God of justice; blessed are all those who wait for him.

—Isaiah 30:18, ESV

but they who wait for the LORD shall renew their strength; they shall mount up with wings like eagles; they shall run and not be weary; they shall walk and not faint.

—Isaiah 40:31, ESV

The LORD is good to those who wait for him, to the soul who seeks him.

—Lamentations 3:25, ESV

But as for me, I will look to the LORD; I will wait for the God of my salvation; my God will hear me.

—Micah 7:7, ESV

And while staying with them he ordered them not to depart from Jerusalem, but to wait for the promise of the Father.

—Acts 1:4, ESV

A MAKING BRAVE PRAYER

Lord, forgive me for breaching the promises I know You've given me. I know You have a purpose for my future. I receive Your promise to me: *"'For I know the plans I have for you,' declares the Lord, 'plans to prosper you and not to harm you, plans to give you hope and a future'"* (Jeremiah 29:11, NIV).

I choose to bide, as long as it takes and as hard as it may be, to receive the fullness of the blessing that comes from placing my trust in You, not in circumstances. I choose to wait for Your miraculous provision, especially when I want to step in and manipulate the problem. I choose to live a life filled with *kairos* moments in the midst of my *chronos* days. Only You are worth waiting for. Only You are the fulfillment of all my best hopes. You will never let me down. You will bring me to my best beautiful outcome. Thank You. Amen.

CONFIDENCE ISN'T WALKING INTO A ROOM WITH YOUR NOSE IN THE AIR, THINKING YOU'RE BETTER THAN EVERYONE ELSE. IT'S WALKING INTO A ROOM AND NOT HAVING TO COMPARE YOURSELF TO ANYONE ELSE IN THE FIRST PLACE.

4. WHEN BRAVE TURNS TO BITTER–LEAH AND RACHEL

Don't Envy Others' Success

Our envy of others devours us most of all.

—Alexander Solzhenitsyn[23]

WHEN OUR DAUGHTER, TASHA, WAS GROWING UP, WE NOTICED SHE HAD a strong value for justice, expressed by her declaring repeatedly, "That's not fair!" She was in a constant battle for equity and righting all the perceived wrongs in her world.

When we were on a girls' trip in New York City, looking for the perfect pair of jeans for her, she kept appearing out of the change room with righteous indignation, saying "I have no hips! That's not fair!"

When she needed extra money for school, her dad gave her a job and allotted her the back office, which she claimed was a human rights violation because it didn't have a window. Again, we heard, "That's not fair!"

Now, as a mother of two young boys, Tasha has seen her body accommodate the beautiful role of nurturing those babies, and I'm sure that while she might yearn for her "no-hip" days, she has received more than she ever dreamed with the opportunity to mother and raise her sons.

When do you get less than you deserve? When do you get more than you ever dreamed? When is life ever fair? Maybe, like me, you feel that sometimes the scales never stay balanced long enough for you to feel like anything is being weighed in your favour. You think you deserve a fair shake, a fair hearing, a fair trial, only to find the scales always seem to be tipped in someone else's favour. They become success stories and you are overlooked yet again.

When I was six years old, I became extremely ill. During the year it took the doctors to diagnose me, I was in the hospital for much of the time, and was put on cortisone to manage my symptoms. Finally, my malfunctioning spleen was removed, which proved to be the solution to the medical issue; however, a year of medication had the side-effect of significant weight gain. I returned to school a year later, looking and feeling different in my body and experiencing the pain of not fitting in because of how I looked.

Was it fair that a vibrant, active six-year-old became a sluggish and introverted seven-year-old with body image trauma because of a medical issue I never asked for?

Years ago, I experienced another tipping of the scales when I was unfairly accused of choosing favourites in a women's mentorship group. One of the young women I was mentoring pointed out—repeatedly—that I was spending more time with one of the other young women; a seed of envy was planted in her.

Unbelievably, we were all grown women who loved Jesus, and yet that need for attention to be allotted fairly was what destroyed the relationships within that group. It was a grief I carried for years while the Lord worked in me—and in the lives of the other women—to bring restoration for some of us, but not all of us. That one particular relationship remains broken.

Sue Monk Kidd, in her book, *The Secret Life of Bees*[24], reminds us: "Nothing is fair in this world. You might as well get that straight right now."

I'm taking more time here to lead us into the story we'll be looking at together of Leah and Rachel, because I believe that if we don't grasp the peril of comparing ourselves to someone else and resenting their success, we're in danger of losing our very identity—and never regaining it.

I only wish I'd been reminded of the words in Proverbs 16:11 earlier: "*The Lord demands accurate scales and balances; he sets the standards for fairness*" (NLT). Really, it's not up to you or me to choose where we are born, our genetic makeup, or the circumstances placed in front of us as challenges. But we can choose how to respond.

God is the only One who created the system of weights and balances. He's the One who created the opportunity for us to keep and maintain truth and justice for the good of others. He appoints, He commands, He approves.

Justice and fairness are significant to God. Why are we okay with submitting to God when it comes to justice or fairness in government and the law, and yet not in our own personal lives? Perhaps we think we know how to balance the personal scales of fairness more than God does.

Injustice and unfairness run in the story of God from Genesis through Revelation. People do the right thing and suffer. People do the wrong thing and don't. Bad people do good things and good people do bad things. God gives and God takes away, doesn't He? Look at Job when he finally realized: *"I came naked from my mother's womb, and I will be naked when I leave. The Lord gave me what I had, and the Lord has taken it away. Praise the name of the Lord!"* (Job 1:21, NLT)

Looking at justice and fairness from God's perspective can help ground us before we get into Leah's and Rachel's story. Here are some principles to keep in mind:

GOD PUT US IN AN ENVIABLE POSITION

Even in our brokenness, while we wait for all things to be restored, we can be assured that all will be put right. I Peter 1:3–6 reminds us:

> *All praise to God, the Father of our Lord Jesus Christ. It is by his great mercy that we have been born again, because God raised Jesus Christ from the dead. Now we live with great expectation, and we have a priceless inheritance—an inheritance that is kept in heaven for you, pure and undefiled, beyond the reach of change and decay. And through your faith, God is protecting you by his power until you receive this salvation, which is ready to be revealed on the last day for all to see.*
>
> *So be truly glad. There is wonderful joy ahead, even though you must endure many trials for a little while.* (NLT)

GOD PLANNED A WAY OUT BEFORE THE PAIN OF ENVY BEGAN

God gave Adam and Eve free will, but even before they took the first bite of the apple and introduced sin into the world, God planned the way out with the promise of Jesus, who was the only One who could take their sin—and ours—and present them holy before God.

GOD'S PLAN INCLUDES PITTING US AGAINST OUR ENEMIES

There are many stories of saints being accused unjustly, or pursued unjustly, and not being able to get away from those who would seek to destroy them because of envy. Look at Saul and David. David was in Saul's household and considered a friend. But because of Saul's jealousy, David had to run for his life for fifteen years. Even Jesus was hated by almost everyone.

GOD'S PLAN INCLUDES OUR ENEMIES BEING THOSE CLOSEST TO US

In Psalm 55:12–14, David reminds us of the great despair of being betrayed by His friends:

> It is not an enemy who taunts me, I could bear that. It is not my foes who so arrogantly insult me—I could have hidden from them. Instead, it is you—my equal, my companion and close friend. What good fellowship we once enjoyed as we walked together to the house of God. (NLT)

Have you ever felt that your greatest pain has been caused by those closest to you? Consider that God allowed it as an opportunity to shape your character.

GOD'S PLAN PUSHES US INTO OUR OWN IDENTITY, NOT SOMEONE ELSE'S

God can put us in uncomfortable situations with those whom we envy so we can find our true identity in Him. He doesn't want us to have what others have; rather, He wants us to find our fulfillment, destiny, and desires met in Him.

GOD PITS US AGAINST OTHERS TO FIND OUR IDENTITY IN HIM

Genesis 29:3 to 30:24 tells the story of Leah and Rachel—the story of two sisters who each envied the other. The rivalry between the two sisters existed because each one wanted what the other had.

The 2009 movie, *Bride Wars*, starred Anne Hathaway and Kate Hudson, playing best friends who turned enemies and competed with each other for the "best wedding." In the end, they both lost. We could give a story of Leah and Rachel a modern-day title, "The Battle of the Brides"—or, even better, "The Battle of the Wives."

Leah wanted Jacob's love.

Rachel wanted Jacob's children.

Eventually, God gave them both what they *wanted*—but what they really *needed* was to know who they were in Him. But they spent so much time in envy and pain, all because they were focused on wanting what belonged to the other.

In Genesis 27, Jacob, the future husband of both women, had already swindled his brother, Esau, out of the birthright, and then he had deceitfully taken away the blessing of their father, Isaac. Esau, having been double-crossed twice, was so angry that he prepared to kill Jacob. When their mother, Rebekah, found out about Esau's plans, she persuaded Isaac to send Jacob up to the City of Haran, where her brother, Laban, lived to find a wife. Jacob left home, headed north, found Laban, and became employed as one of Laban's workers.

Laban had two daughters: Leah (the oldest) and Rachel. Rachel had the body of a goddess and the face of a supermodel; Leah is described as having "weak" eyes. Jacob immediately fell head-over-heels in love with Rachel. He told Laban that he would work seven years for Laban and, as payment, he would get to marry Rachel. Both men shook hands on the deal.

At the end of the seven years, Laban swindled Jacob by switching Leah for Rachel towards the end of the marriage ceremony. He pulled it off by having Leah wear a veil over her face so Laban wouldn't recognize her. Jacob thought he was spending the night with Rachel, but Laban had substituted Leah in her place. Jacob was furious; the swindler had been swindled. He and Laban worked out another deal for another seven years of service. When the seven-year marriage ritual with Leah was complete, Jacob immediately married Rachel.

The seeds of envy and bitterness likely began here, and everyone was affected by Laban's deception. Later, in Genesis 31:15, daughters say this of their father: "*He has reduced our rights to those of foreign women, and after he sold us, he wasted the money you paid him for us*" (NLT). Both women started this story already devalued by a man they had trusted: their father.

The Bible says in Genesis 29:30 that "*Jacob loved Rachel much more than Leah*" (NLT). The words "more than" are not in the original Hebrew text; The Old Testament interpreters added them later. The Bible indicates that Jacob did not love Leah *at all*. Jacob had eyes only for Rachel (the supermodel) and he didn't care about Leah, the plain woman who likely would have needed glasses today.

But upon marrying Jacob, Rachel discovered she was unable to have children; meanwhile, Leah had given birth to four sons: Reuben, Simeon, Levi, and Judah (Genesis 29:31–33).

Not to be outdone, Rachel asked Jacob to sleep with her maid, Bilhah. (This was in line with the custom of the time.) Bilhah gave birth to two boys, whom Rachel named Dan and Naphtali.

This only intensified the rivalry between the two sisters. Leah then asked Jacob to sleep with her maid, Zilpah, and she too gave birth to two sons, Gad and Asher. But this didn't satisfy Leah.

As if to rub more salt into Rachel's wounds, Leah united with Jacob again and gave birth to another two boys and one girl: Issachar, Zebulun, and Dinah (Genesis 30).

In this home, children were used as tools of rivalry and revenge. It wouldn't have been a pleasant—or even a safe—place for those children.

Finally, Rachel gave birth to a son, Joseph (Genesis 30:22–24).

Just when things were looking brighter for Rachel, another twist came. Laban and his sons were getting irritated at how well Jacob was doing with his growing family. Jacob, noting the hostility, decided it was time to do a run again. Leah and Rachel both happily agreed to return to his home with him (Genesis 31).

On the journey back, Rachel gave birth to another son, but she died after childbirth. She called him Ben-oni, which means "son of my sorrow," but Jacob renamed him Benjamin, which means "son of my right hand" (Genesis 35).

I believe that while Jacob thought he loved Rachel, it wasn't evident during this difficult time in Rachel's life. It seems she lacked assurance of Jacob's love. This was a family gone wrong in so many ways.

Two women: one was loved, the other unloved. One had difficulty bearing children, the other's womb was open. Let's look more closely at how they differed:

- Rachel was mostly barren (a sign of God's displeasure).
- Leah bore many children (a sign of God's favour).
- Rachel stole her father's idols and kept them in her tent.
- Leah kept asking God for more sons in the hope that Jacob would love her.
- Rachel traded Jacob to Leah (for a night) for some of Leah's freshly caught geese.
- Leah craved Jacob's love, which he had only for Rachel.
- Rachel was jealous of Leah over her fertility.
- The Bible doesn't say that Leah was *jealous* of Rachel over anything.
- Rachel was unhappy with God closing her womb.
- Leah was happy and rejoiced over her children.
- When Rachel died (after giving birth to Benjamin), Jacob buried her near Bethlehem.
- When Leah died many years later, Jacob buried her next to Abraham and Sarah, and Isaac and Rebekah.

When Jacob was old and dying, he gave his sons instructions to bury him with his forefathers, and next to Leah, giving Leah—not Rachel—much honour. Leah, not Rachel, was buried with Jacob's forefathers. Jacob wanted to be buried next to Leah, not Rachel.

In the end, it was Leah, not Rachel, who was loved. What happened?

Jacob might have started seeing things from God's perspective and seen God's love for Leah. He might have seen that Leah was focused on God, but Rachel wasn't. Thousands of years later, the Messiah would be born through the lineage of Judah, who was Leah's son, not Rachel's. Levi, Leah's son, became the father of the line of Priests.

Leah wasn't blessed with physical beauty, but she was indeed blessed and loved by God.

Leah and Rachel shared:

- A heritage
- A husband
- A home
- A heart that longed for what the other had

Comparison leads to competition and competition leads to control. Rachel was lovely. Leah was unlovely and desired Rachel's beauty. Leah was fruitful. Rachel was barren and desired Leah's fertility.

In Genesis 29:32–35, we get a glimpse into Leah's journey. Each of her four children became a pawn to garner Jacob's love and attention:

> *So Leah became pregnant and gave birth to a son. She named him Reuben, for she said, "The LORD HAS NOTICED MY MISERY, AND NOW MY HUSBAND WILL LOVE ME."*
>
> *SHE SOON BECAME PREGNANT AGAIN AND GAVE BIRTH TO ANOTHER SON. SHE NAMED HIM SIMEON, FOR SHE SAID, "THE LORD HEARD THAT I WAS UNLOVED AND HAS GIVEN ME ANOTHER SON."*
>
> *THEN SHE BECAME PREGNANT A THIRD TIME AND GAVE BIRTH TO ANOTHER SON. HE WAS NAMED LEVI, FOR SHE SAID, "SURELY THIS TIME MY HUSBAND WILL FEEL AFFECTION FOR ME, SINCE I HAVE GIVEN HIM THREE SONS!"*
>
> *ONCE AGAIN LEAH BECAME PREGNANT AND GAVE BIRTH TO ANOTHER SON. SHE NAMED HIM JUDAH, FOR SHE SAID, "NOW I WILL PRAISE THE LORD!" AND THEN SHE STOPPED HAVING CHILDREN.*
>
> —Genesis 29:32–35, NLT

Three children! Yet all Leah could think about was getting Jacob's attention and somehow forcing him to love her. But by the fourth child (Judah), something in Leah changed, and she turned her focus upward to God and began to receive the love He had always offered her.

This is Rachel's reaction while Leah was having children, one after another, and Jacob's follow-up response to Rachel:

When Rachel saw that she wasn't having any children for Jacob, she became jealous of her sister. She pleaded with Jacob, "Give me children, or I'll die!"

Then Jacob became furious with Rachel. "Am I God?" he asked. "He's the one who has kept you from having children!"

—Genesis 30:1–2, NLT

Jacob knew that God was the One who measured out justice. He knew it was in God's hands, not his. I believe Jacob just didn't want to deal with the competing-sister-wives situation anymore. He had loved Rachel so deeply but became fed up and angry, wishing she would just figure out her own issues.

Rachel was barren. Leah was blessed

Rachel was beautiful. Leah was barely seen.

Rachel was broken. Leah was brave.

Rachel's envy cost her true love. Leah's envy cost her sisterhood. In the end, they might've gotten what they wanted, but they lost more in the process.

For many of us, we think we get what we want in the end, but it costs us.

What would have the outcome been if instead of believing "her success robs me of mine," they believed "her success does not diminish mine." In the end, you might think you get what you want, but you end up losing more.

Envy doesn't solve our problems or get us what we want. Envy makes us blind to what we have and miserable because of what we think we lack. When envy is our motivator, we begin measuring our worth based on other people's success. We elevate others because of our jealousy and end up devaluing our own identity and also greatly diminishing our potential to influence. Leah could have risen to her potential and been a noble woman of character had she been comfortable in her own skin and owned her place of influence.

Our temptation to compare distracts us from being who God has called us to be. Rather than focus on what God has purposefully designed us for, we distract ourselves with this clout killer that robs us of leading from a place of security and confidence.[25]

Leah's and Rachel's identity were dependent on diminishing the other's. Leah trusted God, stopped trusting Him, and then found Him again.

Rachel trusted her husband, didn't trust God, and never found trust in anyone again. She had the opportunity to embrace her identity as loved by Jacob and by God, but instead chose inanimate idols as a substitute. *"Rachel stole her father's household idols and took them with her"* (Genesis 31:19b, NLT).

Our secrets keep us sick. Rachel kept the secret of idol theft until her death, and I imagined her as buried clutching her idols, because that's what her identity was reduced to—something perishable. She had everything that was beautiful on the outside, but inside, it was all decay. What goes around, comes around. Deceivers are themselves deceived.

Had she trusted God enough to know that, in the end, all would be made right, would she have made the same choice?

Rachel had access to knowledge of a loving God who had plans for her and her destiny. She could've chosen to believe:

- While you are facing fear and failure, God is securing your future.
- While you are feeling unfavoured, God is making you fertile.
- While you are faking it, God is grounding you in your future identity.

Rachel turned to her father's idols to give her hope. They weren't even hers; she had to steal her hope from someone else. She didn't know who she was and to whom she belonged.

Leah, though, embraced her identity as "beloved" to secure her hope.

In Genesis 30:7–8, we read that Rachel's struggle was with her sister. *"I have had a great struggle with my sister, and I have won."*

But Leah's wrestling was with *God*.

Have you tried to secure your future through manipulation? Have you tried to thwart someone else's success through unforgiveness? Or by punishing them?

Fair fighting is a respectful, structured way of confronting each other on issues causing open or hidden conflict. But because we don't know how to fight fair, we revert to guerilla warfare. Both sisters resorted to deceit and trying to gain control by offering their maids to Jacob to produce children. Leah even "paid" for a night in Jacob's tent by giving Rachel some mandrakes, known for boosting a woman's fertility.

They went back and forth, trying to win Jacob's love by bearing more children; it must've been exhausting. One paraded her beauty in front of the other; the other paraded her children. But one of the sisters was braver than the other.

Rachel completely misunderstood that God eventually opened her womb out of His love for her. She thought He was vindicating her of all of her enmity towards Leah. She was not wholeheartedly committed to serving Him, because as quickly as she praised God for the gift of children, she turned to idols to satisfy her even greater need for identity.

Where did Leah's bravery get her?

Leah, although she became embroiled in the sister-wife battle, never lost her wonder of God's grace in her life.

THE BRAVE TRUTH

The following Scripture is helpful in reminding us that there's always a bigger picture being painted, and a bigger plan than we can often see:

> *Then Job replied to the Lord: "I know that you can do all things; no purpose of yours can be thwarted.*
>
> *You asked, 'Who is this that obscures my plans without knowledge?'*
>
> *Surely I spoke of things I did not understand, things too wonderful for me to know.*
>
> *You said, 'Listen now, and I will speak; I will question you, and you shall answer me.' My ears had heard of you, but now my eyes have seen you. Therefore I despise myself and repent in dust and ashes."*
>
> — Job 42:1–6, NIV

When have you despaired that anything was going to change in your life? When has scrolling image after image on social media left you feeling envious of everyone else's life and what they have, and despising your own? When have you wanted to try anything to manipulate a situation in your favour, or make someone else look bad so you could look good? When have you tried to put on a false mask be someone you're not, just to be loved and accepted?

If you have felt or done any (or all) of these, you might've lost sight of the bigger picture God's asking you to see. Leah couldn't see then that she would be the mother of those in the lineage leading right to Jesus Himself. Rachel didn't see that if she had trusted God to give her what she desired, she wouldn't have had to steal worthless idols.

Do you have possessions or status, or a measure of success that you are tethering to your identity, instead of trusting God to bring you what's best for you in His time?

Here are some principles to keep you focused on the bigger picture, rather than on just the sliver of your life that might not be what you had pictured.

God is faithful in your present while He's focused on your future. Leah's bloodline leads directly to Jesus. Rachel's barrenness turned to blessing when God opened her womb.

God is your best hope for a fair outcome, but you may have to wait until eternity to see it fulfilled. You have no idea today what will happen in your future. But you must believe it will be equitable and fairly measured, and that your faithfulness will bring a harvest of righteousness for you and generations to come.

God has chosen you and will administer justice on your behalf. He will do it in the way He sees fit, and often it won't "feel" fair at all. Sometimes He'll pit you against your enemy. Stay the course. Let justice prevail. While you're in the midst of battle, find your identity in Him.

We are naturally prone to measure how loved we are by how loved others are. But God measures our capacity to receive His love. And no one can love us like He can.

Neither Leah nor Rachel received fully the love they so desperately craved from Jacob. While they were so focused on vying for his love and attention, they lost many opportunities to forge their relationship with God and a closer sister relationship with each other by celebrating each other's victories rather than diminishing them. And in doing so, they left so much on the table.

Perhaps you're married to a man who doesn't love you. Perhaps your spouse fell in love with your beauty, but you couldn't give him children. Perhaps your grown children haven't contacted you for a long time, or friends have betrayed or "ghosted" you. It happens; even with good people.

But where is your focus? Leah's focus was on God, who slowly turned Jacob's heart towards her, and he loved her more than he had ever loved Rachel. While Leah was waiting all those years, she never gave up hope, and God continued to love and bless Leah.

And He will never stop loving you.

Many women desire to be gorgeous like Rachel; to be desired by men. But God wants women to desire *Him*. He wants women with "weak eyes" like Leah, who focus on Him, not the world. You know how painful and tough life really is as you live from day to day. Will you face life and focus your eyes on God (Leah)? Or will you focus inward and on your problems (Rachel)?

I have met this spirit of envy head-on here in this nation. Through Gather Women, we desire to create more opportunities for Canadian women to be visible and use their voice. Although we believe there's room for everyone, culturally, geographically, generationally, and denominationally, some women have expressed fear that there's no room for them. They want to be on the platform, become public figures on social media, and be liked/affirmed. That's fine, but when someone who is a better presenter or writer, or has more of a following, shows up, it can be hard to step back and not be a bit jealous.

Here are some indications that you might be verging on becoming "green with envy."

- You often compare your wealth, status, and appearance, or church affiliation to the people around you.
- It's difficult for you to listen to other people share their success stories.
- You think you deserve more recognition for your accomplishments than you actually receive.
- You worry other people perceive you as a loser.

- It sometimes feels like no matter how hard you try, everyone else seems to be more successful.
- You feel disgust, rather than joy, towards people who are able to achieve their dreams.
- It's hard to be around people who have children who are doing better than yours.
- You feel embarrassed by your lack of success.
- You sometimes imply that you're doing better than you actually are.
- You secretly experience joy when a successful person encounters misfortune.

Even if you agree with just *one* of the above statements, it's time to stop in your tracks and change your gaze from horizontal preoccupation to upward, where God is waiting to lavish His love and favour on you. That's the only antidote to envy.

At Break Forth Canada, one of the largest gatherings at the church in Canada, Gather Women had the opportunity to host a conference for women called "See Her Rise." World-renowned author and speaker Lisa Bevere joined the platform and said something that I remember multiple times every day: "When God chooses to elevate, gives platform to, or raise up another woman, He doesn't withdraw anything from *your* bank account."

Here's what's *not* helpful:

- Chasing after everyone else's dreams
- Imagining how much better everyone else's lives are
- Constantly comparing yourself to everyone around you
- Diminishing other people's achievements
- Treating everyone like they're your direct competition

Here's what *is* helpful:

- Create your own biblical definition of "success"
- Replace negative thoughts that breed resentment with more rational thoughts

- Celebrate other people's accomplishments
- Focus on your unique strengths and opportunities
- Cooperate, rather than compete, with everyone

It's your choice from which list you choose to draw more often. One will take you down a path of self-regret, with worthless idols clutched, enslaved to a false expectation of your worth. The other will take you to the portal of a wide-open path, full of opportunities to raise others up without diminishing yourself, and free to serve, knowing you have inherent value to God as *His creation*.

We are meant to champion each other and create spaces for others to rise. When one rises, we all rise. Collaboration must always trump competition. I have seen and experienced competition up close and personal, and I can tell you that it harms the beauty of what the church is supposed to be representing: unity through diversity.

I have two sisters. If I could, I would trade elements of my personality and looks and in exchange for their talents and gorgeous looks! But we have learned to celebrate each other's successes and comfort each other in our sorrows.

The story of the competition between Leah and Rachel is a tale of two sisters. Which one will you choose to be? *Where will your bravery get you?* Where will it get you even amid unbearable circumstances in which everything you wanted is paraded in front of you daily?

Will you be brave enough to trust God that He's writing your story for future generations? Will they see a woman willing to stay and trust God whether He gives and takes away from you, and whether He gives and takes away from someone else?

Don't envy someone else's success. Focus on all that is yours in Christ.

STUDY QUESTIONS

In what ways are you "faking it," like Leah? To whom are you comparing yourself, and why?

In what ways are you competing for someone else's story?

In what ways is comparison raising the volume on your "unfair" declaration? How are you trying to control a fair outcome?

Where are you finding your identity? In trusting God to measure out His best version of "fair?" Or are you fighting for someone else's?

A MAKING BRAVE PRAYER

My true identity is as a Child of God. This is the identity I have to accept. Once I have claimed it and settled it, I can live in a world that gives me much joy as well as pain. I can receive the praise as well as the blame that comes to me as an opportunity for strengthening my basic identity, because the identity that makes me free is anchored beyond all human praise and blame. I belong to God, and it is as a Child of God that I am sent into the world.[26] (adapted from Henri Nouwen)

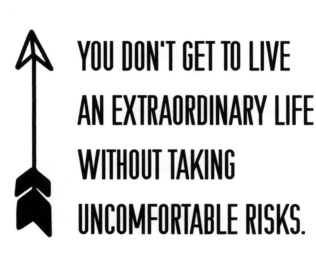

YOU DON'T GET TO LIVE AN EXTRAORDINARY LIFE WITHOUT TAKING UNCOMFORTABLE RISKS.

5. BRAVER THAN BRAVE CAN BE—JOCHEBED AND RAHAB

Don't Fear Taking Calculated Risks

Life is either a daring adventure or nothing at all.

—Helen Keller[27]

JOANNA'S STORY:

I've never heard anyone say that they wish they'd been less brave in a situation. Our regrets often come from moments where we'd wanted more courage, not less.

Courage to tell them how we really feel. Bravery to try a new thing. Fortitude to end something that's run its course.

I haven't made any significant life decision without a good dose of bravery. Bravery has served me well as I've stepped into the big wide unknowns in my life.

I was brave enough to end a relationship that had turned toxic after many years together. I needed to be brave when I chose to live abroad in France, where I knew no one and could barely speak the language. I needed courage to say "Yes" to Jesus when He asked me to leave a city and community I loved to take on an enormous challenge of skill and character at a church back in my hometown. More recently, I needed bravery to go out on my own as I grew my own business without those safety nets of salaries, retirement funds, and health insurance.

It's also important that I don't give you the wrong impression. I'm not all bravery and fearlessness. Generally, I have wrestled with anxiety for as long as I can remember. I used to be sick and throw up every time I spoke publicly or got on an airplane.

Although I've done a lot of both in my life, I was wracked with fear about it for decades. Anyone who's worked or travelled with me knows I used to be notorious for this. I carried those airplane sickness bags around with me for a while. It led me to lean on God and a good professional counsellor to get more freedom and healing in my life.

In the midst of the fears of anxiety that come and go, I have also determined to never let it stop me from what I felt were the dreams and calling on my life. I may have anxiety, but it will not be the boss of me. I want bravery to win. Anxiety does not serve me well, and it doesn't add a single hour to my life… in fact, I'm quite sure I've lost some years of my life because of it. Year by year, I'm being healed and freed up to be a more brave woman.

I know I have never regretted one brave moment. God has used them all to make me the kind of person that walks more closely with him and trusts him more fully with my future. As Amanda Cook sings, "He makes me brave."

My friends, whatever is in front of you today, let bravery be the boss of you.[28]

Scared is what you *feel*. Brave is what you *do*.

We come from a long line of women who have put their brave on in defining moments, whether scared or not. One of those women was Moses' mother, Jochebed. We read about her in Exodus 2:1–3:

> *Now a man of the tribe of Levi married a Levite woman, and she became pregnant and gave birth to a son. When she saw that he was a fine child, she hid him for three months. But when she could hide him no longer, she got a papyrus basket for him and coated it with tar and pitch. Then she placed the child in it and put it among the reeds along the bank of the Nile.* (NIV)

I used to hear this story in Sunday school; eventually, after hearing it enough times, I started thinking, "Okay, so she put Moses in a basket and placed it in the Nile?"

Excuse me, but she did *what*?

She put Moses—her most precious possession—in a basket and placed it in the Nile River! She *did* that? Would *I* have done that? I doubt it. Would *you* have done that?

Who was this brave woman, and where did she come from?

Exodus 6:20 tells us that "*Amram married his father's sister Jochebed, who bore him Aaron and Moses*" (NIV). Numbers 26:59 goes on to say, "*The name of Amram's wife was Jochebed, a descendant of Levi, who was born to the Levites in Egypt. To Amram she bore Aaron, Moses and their sister Miriam*" (NIV).

Jochebed came from the right tribe (descendant of Levi), married the right man (a Levite), and served the right God. She had a godly, rich heritage and knew God's promises. She married into the right family, though a younger man, her nephew—but this was not unusual in the time. She had already given birth to two potential world changers: Aaron and Miriam.

When Moses was born, Jochebed knew she had a gifted, unique child. Scripture tells us Moses was not ordinary; he was *tov*, the Hebrew word for "good" and "beautiful." It's the same word used in the creation account when God looked at all He had made and said it was "very good."

Tov conveys the possibility that Jochebed sensed something was special about her new baby boy. Maybe she believed God would use Him to fulfill the Promise from Joseph's mouth in Genesis 50:24: "*God will surely come to help you and lead you out of this land of Egypt. He will bring you back to the land He solemnly promised to give to Abraham, to Isaac, and to Jacob*" (NLT).

But a rescue was needed. Pharaoh was adamant that all Hebrew baby boys should be killed, as the Israelites in Egypt were multiplying too fast and becoming a serious threat to those in power.

Jochebed was facing what all of her Hebrew friends were facing: the killing off of their infant sons. As a woman of faith, she knew God's promise. So she chose to act.

She hid him for *three months*. Imagine keeping your child quiet, day after day, hiding him in secret, in fear that any day you could be found out if he cried out a little too loudly.

She desperately wanted to keep him and protect him, but knew she had to surrender him. I can only imagine the wrestling that went on in her soul as, day after day, she prepared her basket of surrender and strategized on how she could release him into God's hands. Think about what that might feel like—the letting go, the surrender into an unknown future full of danger.

She must have known that God was good—that He could be trusted. It took one defining moment, one act of surrender, one act of bravery that changed the trajectory of history. That moment was the actual surrender of Moses in the basket, into the Nile. It required kneeling down and letting go.

What have we learned about Jochebed?

- Jochebed was Moses' mother
- She was "holy"—her name contains a form of Jehovah and means "glory"
- Jochebed lived a life of faith and expectation
- She was mentioned with Amram in Hebrews 11:23

Later in Exodus, Moses was rescued by Pharaoh's daughter and brought up to the palace, where he was raised. After an altercation during which Moses killed an Egyptian, in fear and confusion regarding his identity, he ran away to the desert for forty years to find himself. He met God in the burning bush, and returned with a renewed purpose and God's presence to lead His people out of Egypt after four hundred years of slavery.

Moses died not entering the Promised Land that he had been promised. Before he died, the baton of leadership was passed on to Joshua, who, at age eighty, was ready to claim the land the Israelites were seeking. He spent spies into Jericho to check out the city.

This is where the story of Rahab comes into play. In defiance of the king, she hid the spies under some grain on her roof, and when asked about their whereabouts, she lied to protect them, claiming she didn't know who they were, and that they had left.

Rahab was a woman *without* a legacy of faith, unlike Jochebed. Yet she had heard of God and told the spies: in Joshua 2:9, 12:

"I know the Lord has given you this land … The Lord your God is the supreme God of the heavens above and the earth below.

Now swear to me by the Lord that you will be kind to me and my family since I have helped you. Give me some guarantee that when Jericho is conquered, you will let me live, along with my father and mother, my brothers and sisters, and all their families.

—Joshua 2:9, 12–13, NLT

The spies made the promise, asking her to leave a scarlet cord hanging from her window so that when they came to conquer Jericho, they would save her and her family.

Rahab had lived a life of failed expectations. No one in her life had truly loved her. She did not have the perfect bloodline of Jochebed. She had no husband, no children, no future. She *did* have a reputation as a harlot— used by many and loved by none.

Yet she was brave, staking her life and the life of her family members on a promise with spies she didn't know based on a God she'd never met.

What have we learned about Rahab?

- Rahab was a mother in the line of the Messiah
- Rahab was not holy, but a harlot
- Rahab lived a life of failed expectations
- Rahab is mentioned in the New Testament three times, each time called a harlot, yet each time covered in grace

Rahab had heard of the miracles the Lord had done for Israel. She believed His promises would be fulfilled, and Jericho would be conquered.

In a very real sense, Rahab became like the Levite that Jochebed was, adopted into this family. In dropping the scarlet cord, like the blood upon the doorpost at the Passover, she brought to remembrance the sinner's security under Christ's atoning blood. The same cord Rahab used to save the spies was to be used for her own safety.

The "line" or cord was spun of threads dyed a deep, bright scarlet colour. The use of scarlet was part of the Levitical rites, those closely connected with the idea of putting away of sin and its consequences.

So what do we do with these two seemingly opposite women? One steeped in a heritage of faith, one adopted into faith. One living a life of faith expectation, one with failed expectations.

The following diagram shows how these two brave women's stories connect and intertwine:

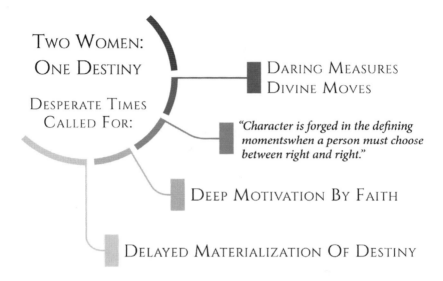

TWO WOMEN:
ONE DESTINY

DESPERATE TIMES
CALLED FOR:

DARING MEASURES
DIVINE MOVES

"Character is forged in the defining momentswhen a person must choose between right and right."

DEEP MOTIVATION BY FAITH

DELAYED MATERIALIZATION OF DESTINY

For both Jochebed and Rahab, while the rest of their people waited in fear, doing nothing was not an option. Neither of then conformed to the culture of their day. They were the only women in their respective contexts who thought and acted differently. They strategized and hid what would bring redemption; Jochebed hid Moses, Rahab hid the spies. One of the spies was Salmon, whom she later married; out of their union came Boaz, a type of the Kinsmen Redeemer who led directly to Jesus.

At some point, both women had to step into their brave moment and make a bold move. It took seconds to surrender the basket. It took seconds to drop the cord. But they did it. Everything changed for Israel, and everything changed for Rahab and the generations to come that led to Christ.

They both lied to the governing powers. Jochebed hid her child, which was against the law. Rahab lied to the King's face. Both women took calculated risks and strategized their brave moves, rather than leaving their lives to chance.

Character is formed in the defining moments when a person must choose *right* over *right*. How do we choose right over right in defining moments? We tend to want our mission clearly spelled out for us regarding what the will of God is in moments like this. Does bravery mean choosing life over death?

When life is on the line, God will choose to forge your character, rather than allowing your context to define you.

Both women were motivated by faith. Jochebed's faith was secure through her priestly bloodline. Rahab's faith was just a seed, yet she acted in a way that had priestly significance. Both women had to wait to see their destiny materialize, and they had no idea that you and I would be reading their stories and being inspired by their brave moves.

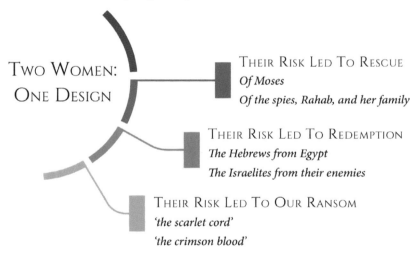

Two Women: One Design

Their Risk Led To Rescue
Of Moses
Of the spies, Rahab, and her family

Their Risk Led To Redemption
The Hebrews from Egypt
The Israelites from their enemies

Their Risk Led To Our Ransom
'the scarlet cord'
'the crimson blood'

Do you find yourself in either of their stories?

As a girl, I always believed I was the one who could be counted on to show up with some brave "swagger" on. I would've told you that I was the brave one among my friends—brave enough to hang from the monkey bars upside down and the last one to admit defeat. My mental image of myself was the Wonder Woman over whom I had fawned in comic books. I was like her—gloriously fearless. I could picture myself adorned with long, flowing hair, a sword in one hand and a shield in the other. I was *that girl*.

Every summer, my parents would take us to British Columbia's hot springs, and I spent my days in the water and diving multiple times off of the diving board—the higher, the better. I was *fearless* in those days.

But somewhere along the way, I lost my brave.

At forty years old, when we returned as a family to the hot springs, I saw that diving board and determined I still had enough brave in me to do a return performance. So, with my family chanting and a growing number of voices chanting, "Cath-ie, Cath-ie, Cath-ie!" I put on my middle-aged swagger and with thighs jiggling, began my ascent up the diving board ladder. I reached the top and dared the skinny adolescent boys already lined up to get out of my way, because I was coming to give the crowd what they wanted. I walked confidently to the edge of the diving board and looked down.

It was far. The water was deep. I lost my nerve. I took a few steps back and walked forward to the edge again. Still too far down, still too deep. I took a few steps back and kept backing up… all the way down the stairs. In fear and shame, and to the disappointment of cheering fans, I just couldn't take the dive. I came back later when the pool had cleared out and dove in, but I'd missed my opportunity to make my brave moment when it mattered.

So often we think brave thoughts but can't actually do the brave thing. And I wonder if our desires to do brave things are often overcome by debilitating fear when faced with stepping into a brave moment.

I took a risk on the diving board that day, and it cost me shame. I've also taken bigger risks that have cost me sacrifice, reputation, ridicule, and rejection.

What's the biggest risk you've ever taken? What did it cost you? Your answer to this will either confirm that you're braver than you think or bring you face-to-face with your failure and shame that when it counted, you couldn't do the hard thing.

Sometimes our inability to act is when we are relying on our own skill and our own ability. It is in the moments where everything seems impossible, that we need the power of God to step in and make our brave possible.

MAKING YOUR BRAVE WAY FORWARD

Sometimes, courage is showing up and letting yourself be seen. Renowned author Brené Brown, in her book, *Daring Greatly,* shares the following quote from Teddy Roosevelt:

> It is not the critic who counts; not the woman who points out how the strong man stumbles, or where the doer of deeds could have done them better. The credit belongs to the woman who is actually in the arena, whose face is marred by dust and sweat and blood; who strives valiantly; who errs, who comes short again and again, because there is no effort without error and shortcoming; but who does actually strive to do the deeds; who knows great enthusiasms, the great devotions; who spends herself in a worthy cause; who at the best knows in the end the triumph of high achievement, and who at the worst, if she fails, at least fails while daring greatly.[29]

Courage means getting in the ring and daring greatly in your own life, rather than being a spectator. Courage almost always calls for *action.*

Jochebed could've let her story unfold and prayed that Moses would not be found by King Herod. *But she chose to act* and released him into the Nile in the basket she had handcrafted. She must've been terrified.

Rahab could've let her story unfold and prayed that she would escape the destruction of Jericho. *But she chose to act* and strategized a plan based on a promise by dropping a scarlet cord. She must've been terrified.

What makes *you* scared? I made a list of some of the most debilitating fears that women I coach struggle with:

- Fear of failure
- Fear of death
- Fear of rejection
- Fear of ridicule
- Fear of being along
- Fear of disappointment

- Fear of scarcity
- Fear of pain
- Fear of the unknown
- Fear of losing your freedom
- Fear of not being enough

To be able to face our fear head-on and move into our brave moments, we need God's help. We must ask the same two questions Eve and Sarah asked God in their defining moments: "God, are You *good*? Are You *able*?"

What we choose to believe about the answers will either propel us forward or move us back into our cocoons of safety and little or no risk.

You might sense God calling you to a brave moment. A conversation He's nudging you to have that could risk either restoring or ending a friendship. A doctor's appointment to make to find out if that nagging pain is minor or a serious medical issue. A call to the bank manager to see if it's possible to refinance your mortgage or if it's time to move. An application to secure an interview for a new job, bringing with it the risk of being rejected again.

There's a piece of our heart that beats in anticipation of what's possible on the other side of fear. There's often a louder, more insistent voice drowning out our feeble cry to step into our brave.

It's the voice that challenges God: "Prove that You're going to come through for me. If I step out, promise me I won't fail, and I won't feel shame if my risk doesn't pay off."

If this voice gets its way, and we can't hear God's voice, our mounting fear takes over our beating heart's desire to make brave moves.

We don't always know how the story will end. The fear of not having our questions answered before we step into our brave moments paralyzes us.

Check in with yourself to gauge whether you're a natural risktaker, or whether you're more risk-averse than you think. If you understand that you might be avoiding taking risks that could help you move forward in your destiny because of fear, that could be the first step in moving through the fear, calculating the risk, and making the choice to act boldly.

Check in with yourself on the following statements:

- You struggle to make important decisions in your life.
- You spend a lot of time daydreaming about what you'd like to do, but you don't take action.
- You impulsively make a decision because thinking about the decision is just too anxiety-provoking.
- You often think you could be doing a lot more adventurous and exciting things in life, but your fear holds you back.
- You think about taking a risk, but only imagine the worst-case scenario and choose not to take the chance.
- You allow other people to make decisions for you, so you don't have to make them.
- You avoid risks in some areas of your life—social, financial, physical, spiritual—because you're afraid of the outcome.
- You tend to base decisions on your level of fear. If you're a little afraid, you might do something. But, if you're very afraid, you decide taking the risk is unwise.
- You think that outcomes are largely dependent on luck, not on your skill or God's participation.

Knowing yourself and how you tend to respond to risk and fear will help you understand why you play it safe.

I know I'm comfortable with risk, but I also like to have one hundred percent confirmation from God that my decision is the right one. Sometimes I have received resounding, clear affirmation by His grace. But for most of my decisions, I moved forward, even when I was only seventy-five percent sure it was the right decision; otherwise, I'd never do anything while waiting for the final twenty-five percent to kick in. I would be stuck in uncertainty forever.

I needed this self-awareness when I and several other brave women stepped out to launch Gather Women in Canada to connect women coast to coast. We are the second-largest nation in the world, with a small population of thirty-seven million and plenty of distance between us.

We wanted to explore the question: "What would it look like if women of faith in Canada were stronger together through a connected coast-to-coast infrastructure?"

But my personal fear was so overwhelming that I didn't want to admit I had waited years for someone else—"the right woman"—to step up and start something. I thought my season for full-on ministry was over. So, with other women sensing with me that it was the time to move, we gathered women. I was *sure*, but not "that" sure.

I still wonder how God has brought us this far, but I wonder even more where He'll take us as a movement—I wonder about His heart for His daughters in this nation. Every time we have a national gathering, or launch a new initiative, such as our HerInfluence podcast, it's a risk. But it's a calculated risk.

We can sit still and do nothing… *or* make the best decisions we can with the information we have and move forward. Canada's church and culture won't be transformed on its own. God can do it, of course, but when He whispers the call to rise and participate in His plans, you stand and raise your hand—whether you're scared or not, whether you believe it's your season or not.

My dear, anointed friend, Helen Burns, pastor of Relate Church in Surrey, B.C., with her husband, inspires me every time I hear her speak. She reminds women that she has her hand raised for Canada, and that she's raising our hands, as well. She believes that as we respond to the call to gather, God is doing and will do an even greater transformational work across the nation, through our women. Helen is a natural risk-taker, but not an unwise one.

And so it was with both Jochebed and Rahab. They took calculated risks, but did so in the fear and wisdom of God. We also have the power of the Holy Spirit to enable, guide, and empower us with all we need to create bold moves.

I've had more than my share of fearful moments, hiding in the dark, and have asked God in the desperate blackness, "When did You ever have to risk anything?"

We were reminded in the first chapter that God made His brave known to us by risking *everything*.

Though he was God, he did not think of equality with God as something to cling to.

> *Instead, he gave up his divine privileges; he took the humble position of a slave and was born as a human being. When he appeared in human form, he humbled himself in obedience to God and died a criminal's death on a cross.*
>
> —Philippians 2:6–8, NLT

The God we serve shows that He's willing to risk everything out of love for us. Does that encourage you to live out your brave?

THE BRAVE TRUTH

Consider some of the truths that can be taken from the stories of Jochebed and Rahab. How will these truths inspire you to live your brave life? Here's what I learned as I leaned into their stories:

- Seasoned bravery comes with a legacy of battles endured, engaged, and won.[30]
- Brave is determined in the fire, in the lion's den, in the baskets of surrender, in the scarlet cords of release.
- *You* have a Hebrews 11 story… you are marked brave when you don't quit, when you stay the course and come out the other side.
- There's no bravery unless you are prepared to be vulnerable and risk everything.
- God calls both those with a respectable past and a reprehensible reputation to move His plans forward.
- *God used women who risked everything* to set into motion the destiny of His chosen people.
- *God honoured women who risked everything* by recording their before-and-after stories.
- God might be calling you in a hinge moment to risk everything for an "after" you don't yet see.
- Do you believe that you can surrender everything to gain everything, even if you can't see it? What's the basket you need to release into the waters?

- What's the cord of surrender you need to release to move into your future?
- What are you displaying as an act of your faith?

It takes action to change the future. It just doesn't work to only *think* brave. Are you willing to make your brave move by *acting* brave to propel you into your future and propel future generations into theirs? That's how it works. Your brave moments inspire others.

Remember, scared is what you *feel*. Brave is what you *do*.

We're walking in a sea of red. There is a beautiful red carpet rolled out for us, made possible by women who came before us and dropped their red cords of surrender and sacrificed their most precious baskets into the unknown. In their brave moments, they had no idea that we would be inspired by their stories to be brave in our bold moments, here and now.

May you have the insight and be given the grace to look deep into the stories of these women and embrace the truths that will help you live your brave moments. Don't fear taking calculated risks. Future generations are waiting for you, are indeed counting on you, to make your brave count.

STUDY QUESTIONS

1. How do you resonate with Jochebed's story? Have you experienced some of the loss she might've been feeling?
2. When did you know you had no choice but to take a big risk? What was the outcome?
3. How do you resonate with Rahab's story? Do you believe your life can be used to ransom the generations to come?
4. How do you feel about the fact that Jesus came directly through Rahab's lineage?
5. Is it easier for you to think brave thoughts rather than dare to put your faith into action?
6. What will you take away from today's lesson? What message do you think God is speaking specifically to you?

A MAKING BRAVE PRAYER

Lord, forgive me for not being brave when I know You make me brave. I know You call me to take action through my biggest fears. I know that you risked everything so that I could gain everything. I know you haven't given me a spirit of fear, but of power and love and self-control. I can be brave because I know You will never leave me nor forsake me.

I choose to risk everything for You and trust You—not my fear—with the outcomes of my brave choices that I can't see.

You took the biggest risk when You chose me, called me by name, and gave me a hope, a future. Help me make my brave moments this week. I will surrender my basket, and let down my scarlet cord for Your sake. You are my best hope. Thank You. Amen.

TO DARE IS TO LOSE ONE'S FOOTING MOMENTARILY. TO NOT DARE IS TO LOSE ONESELF.

—SOREN KIERKEGAARD[31]

6. A BRAVE VALOUR-RUTH

Don't Be Scared of Change

"Go back?" he thought. "No good at all! Go sideways? Impossible! Go forward? Only thing to do! On we go!" So up he got, and trotted along with his little sword held in front of him and one hand feeling the wall, and his heart all of a patter and a pitter.
—J. R. R. Tolkien, *The Hobbit*[32]

VANESSA'S STORY:

Crazy, or called, or a little bit of both?

As I was about to turn forty years old, our family (husband of twenty years, plus four gorgeous daughters ranging from five years old to the teens) heard a clear invitation from God to move countries, to leave the family and friends we loved, to sell everything we owned, and to pioneer a church in a city we had never been to with people we didn't know.

In church-planting terms, it's called "parachuting" into a place. I don't know if it ever felt as glorious as parachuting. That image evokes the lovely feeling of getting an overview and relaxing up in the air before landing.

I would call it being ignited and launched like an old-school canon. Landing with weightiness and not necessarily with ease and comfort.

Before we left Australia, I remember walking down the road and saying to the Lord, "Will You just hold my hand? I need to know You are with me. I can be brave if You are with me." I realized this wasn't an invitation to somewhere, it was to Someone—Jesus Himself.

Jesus said "COME" 265 times in his life (recorded).

The invitation from Jesus is a request for our presence and participation. It's not to another country. It's to Him. Wherever brave takes us.

The definition of COME:

- To advance towards the person speaking (His voice is calling if we listen for it)
- To move into view (I love this… maybe some of you have felt unnoticed and now it's time for Jesus to speak over you ("I SEE YOU"))
- To originate (what a crazy thought that we journey towards our original intended purpose at creation when we draw near to Jesus)
- To be within a certain range of closeness (our invitation)
- To be available and obtainable (brave might mean being present where you are)
- To show up or appear (bravery is often just showing up)
- To recover or revive (beautiful)

On the last and greatest day of the festival, Jesus stood and said in a loud voice, "Let anyone who is thirsty come to me and drink. Whoever believes in me, as Scripture has said, rivers of living water will flow from within them.

—John 7:37—38, NIV

Maybe that's what a calling is—no more and no less than responding to His "Come to Me."

Brave is a responding "Yes" when He calls your name.

When my daughter, Sahara Justice, was learning how to walk, I found the most powerful way I got her to respond and actually move was not to get behind her but instead come in front of her, get down on her little level and CALL HER NAME.

As she heard me calling her name, she found the courage and the confidence to walk towards me.

Living our calling means responding to our name being called. This is what "calling" means to me.

This is also what "crazy" means to the world. This is what brave means. Trust me. Your brave will have been misunderstood. You will grieve the loss of those who don't like your "yes." And your brave will require strength for the journey. It's been the most terrifying, heartbreaking, and fulfilling time of our life.

So I say, of church planting or any courageous "yes" to Jesus, is it craziness or is it calling… or could it be a little bit of both?

It's my heartfelt prayer that you find the same courage when your own name is being called. Crazy, yes! Called, yes! Courageous, yes![33]

One of my favourite TV shows was "Project Runway." I loved seeing the talent of each unique designer as they competed weekly to win the best clothing design. Each week, at the end of the show, hostess Heidi Klum let the designers know that one of them would be the winner, and one of them would be "out."

This is often true in life, isn't it? One day you're in, the next, you're out. We all want to be "in"—in the inner circle, in the right place, at the right time. We try to strategize to be in the right room with the right people. When social media show us that other people have gathered and we were not invited to the party, we become overwhelmed with FOMO (fear of missing out) and jealousy. We wonder what could've happened if had been there, whom we might've met, how our loves could've changed, etc.

We forget that God often uses the wrong woman at the wrong place at the wrong time. If she's open to His leading, as in Vanessa's story, God will move her from one nation to another to fulfill His purposes.

I didn't move nations, but when I got married, moving from Western to Eastern Canada felt like moving to another country. I was a girl always up for an adventure and didn't realize until a few months into my married life in Ontario that my Prairie girl heart was homesick. One of my first questions to my new husband was, "When is everyone coming over?"—because

I had grown up in a home with an open door and homemade perogies ready to serve anyone who dropped by. It felt different to be in an environment where people generally didn't just drop in. I definitely felt "out."

I was without my people. My family members were mostly three thousand miles away and there was no way to connect other than through letters or phone calls back then.

I was without my career. I had been a music teacher in Alberta; moving to Ontario was a transition in terms of finding a new teaching role.

I was without my dreams. I had planned to be the best music educator in the Prairies and gave all that up to move to Ontario.

I had no idea that eventually, I would be without my voice. I tried to conform to the new reality and family I was becoming part of, but it was so much different from how I had been raised. I slowly began to try to please others more than I could stay true to myself; after a few years, I wondered whom I'd become.

I have such an affinity for Ruth of the Old Testament. She'd have been voted "least likely to be voted into the family of God." Yet her story beautifully portrays how she—a foreigner, Moabitess, and widow—was beautifully grafted into the centre of God's family, in a very unique, if not slightly scandalous, way. She was out, then she was in. What I love most is that Jesus came from her family line, and she became a pivotal player in God's family.

As with many of the biblical stories, Ruth's life reads like a soap opera. If you wanted to give each chapter in the book a title, it may be as follows:

Chapter One: Sorrow
Chapter Two: Strategy
Chapter Three: Scandal
Chapter Four: Seed

We read the stunning story of Ruth during the time of the judges when there was a famine, particularly in Judah. Elimelech, his wife Naomi, and their sons Mahlon and Chilion left Bethlehem and moved to nearby country Moab. Elimelech died, and the sons married two Moabite women: Mahlon married Ruth; Chilion, Orpah.

Tragically, ten years later, both of Naomi's sons died and the three women were left on their own.

Ruth was one-of-a-kind because she wasn't born into a family with a legacy; rather, she was from a culture that had a legacy of enmity with God's people.

Yet, she has a starring role in a story that starts with her being outside the main setting.

Ruth was a woman of courage. The root of "courage," is *cor,* the Latin word for "heart." In one of its earliest forms, "courage" meant "to speak one's mind by telling all one's heart."

Ruth was a woman of courageous valour.

Naomi heard of improvements back home in Judah, mostly in terms of the famine easing up, and decided it was time to return. The threesome set out before Naomi realized she needed to release both her daughters-in-law to stay in their homeland and prayed that they would remarry.

Both insisted they would return to Judah with Naomi, and through tears, Orpah kissed her goodbye. But Ruth insisted on carrying on with Naomi, citing the words she became famous for:

> *Where you go I will go, and where you stay I will stay. Your people will be my people and your God my God. Where you die I will die, and there I will be buried. May the Lord deal with me, be it ever so severely, if even death separates you and me.*
>
> —Ruth 1: 16b–17, NIV

Naomi could not say no to the conviction in Ruth's voice.

Where did bravery get Ruth?

Ruth stood out from all of the other Moabite women, including her sister-in-law, Orpah, who chose to stay in their culture, which included worshipping idols.

Ruth is characterized by her courage in the following ways:

RUTH CHOSE COURAGE OVER CULTURE

She chose to leave behind her culture in order to immerse herself in her new world. Her first adventure of this brave step was meeting Boaz.

> *Now Naomi had a relative on her husband's side, a man of standing from the clan of Elimelek, whose name was Boaz. And Ruth the Moabite said to Naomi, "Let me go to the fields and pick up the leftover grain behind anyone whose eyes I find favor." Naomi said to her, "Go ahead, my daughter."*
>
> —Ruth 1:1–2, NIV

Picking up leftover grain was the custom of the day, but Ruth knew that she would immediately be identified as different from any other woman gathering up the leftovers because she was still, culturally, a Moabite. Would there be competition in the field, or even enmity towards her? For Ruth, just showing up was a huge step of courage.

One reason I love Canada is that I believe God is bringing the nations here from all over the world. It is a beautiful tapestry of all of those who will be represented when followers of Christ gather at the feast in eternity with Jesus as the host.

After this I looked, and there before me was a great multitude that no one could count, from every nation, tribe, people and language, standing before the throne and before the Lamb. They were wearing white robes and were holding palm branches in their hands. (Revelation 7:9, NIV)

So often we want to hang on to our culture and the traditions associated with it and elevate traditions above obedience to Christ. Ruth was courageous enough to be able to walk away from her cultural home, but stand firm in hew new country, knowing she would be identified as a foreigner.

RUTH CHOSE COURAGE OVER CONTEXT

Ruth 2:19–21 tells the story of how Ruth went to the field to gather the barley and then beat the grain from it in the evening.

Where do you expect God to find you and elevate you to a position of honour? Certainly not on the threshing floor, nor hidden in the sheaves of wheat, bent over, gathering grain.

We tend to think we need to be in the right place to be seen and noticed in order to get invited to take our place in building God's kingdom. This is far from the truth. God placed Ruth in a less-than-desirable context and Boaz, her future Kinsmen Redeemer, found her there. She didn't parade herself in front of him to be noticed.

RUTH CHOSE COURAGE OVER COMFORT

Ruth 3:3–4 continues with the story of how Naomi coached Ruth to leverage the situation.

How comfortable would you feel dressing up on your mother-in-law's instruction and then going to an older man's threshing floor and laying at his feet? Although it was a custom in the day to do this, if a couple were going to be married, the scandal in this action was that Ruth was quite young and Boaz, much older. She was also a foreigner, and for her, this was a brazen move. Ruth needed courage to put herself out there and make the move, for her sake and the sake of her mother-in-law, securing both their futures.

We often don't want to do the things God might be calling us to because they make us uncomfortable or put us in a position of risking our reputation. Ruth had the strength of character to choose courage over any discomfort she would have felt in that moment.

RUTH CHOSE COURAGE OVER CONFORMITY

Rather than trying to "get her man" with being obvious and using womanly charms, as many women in that day would've done, Ruth chose to use such a unique, yet God-honouring strategy.

What makes Ruth so unique?

The Hebrew words used in Ruth to describe her are *eshet chayil*, which means "woman of valour." It also means to have power, strength, resources, and wisdom. *Eshet* (*smichut*) comes from *isha* and means *woman, feminine*. Ruth is depicted as a powerful woman. Throughout a book of the Bible completely devoted to her story, we see these character qualities in her: Ruth, as *eshet chayil*, is a woman of:

- Valour
- Strength
- Power
- Wisdom
- Resources
- Strategy

The word *chayil* is used three times in the Book of Ruth.

In Ruth 2:1 and Ruth 4:11, the word is translated as "wealth" and is used in reference to Boaz as a man of wealth and strength. But in Ruth 3:1, the word is translated as "excellence" or "virtue" and is used by Boaz in describing Ruth.

How Ruth exhibits her valour is through her strength of character.

Ruth's *internal* identity didn't depend on her external circumstances. In fact, for being singled out as the "foreigner," the one who didn't belong, she was actually the one with the *most secure* identity.

> **VALOUR ISN'T ABOUT WHAT YOU DO, BUT HOW YOU DO IT.**

Here is Ruth's external reality: She was a woman without a husband, without a home, without options. Where did Ruth's bravery get her when her back was up against the wall and she was out of options?

Boaz redeemed Ruth from a marriage to another family member who would have had first rights to her, and Naomi's property. Along with the land, he gained Ruth. The blessing came from all of the elders and the community to Ruth—the foreigner who didn't belong in that world.

In Ruth 4:11b–12, we read:

> *"We are witnesses! May the Lord make this woman who is coming into your home like Rachel and Leah, from whom all the nation of Israel descended! May you prosper in Ephrathah and be famous in Bethlehem. And may the Lord give you descendants by this young*

woman who will be like those of our ancestor Perez, the son of Tamar and Judah." (NLT)

This is the seed—the promise of the future—and the reference to Jesus, the ultimate Kinsmen Redeemer.

Where does your bravery get you when you are out of options?

When you choose to act out of the courage of your convictions rather than cowardice and a fear that nothing will ever change, you create the possibility for new opportunities to open up. You have no idea what the future will hold and what will come from your courage.

THE BRAVERY OF THE PROVERBS 31 WOMAN

In May 2019, the world lost a brave woman and a beautiful writer, Rachel Held Evans. I'll never forget what she wrote about busting some of the myths around the Proverbs 31 woman:

"The woman described in Proverbs 31 is not some ideal that exists out there. She is present in each one of us when we do even the smallest things with valour."[34]

The Proverbs 31 woman shares the same descriptor as Ruth—*eshet chayil*.

A woman of valour who can find?

—Proverbs 31:10[35]

She girds herself with strength [spiritual, mental and physical fitness for her God-given task] and makes her arms strong and firm.

—Proverbs 31:17, AMPC

Strength and dignity are her clothing and her position is strong and secure.

—Proverbs 31:25a, AMPC

We might want to hate this woman, but instead, we should be looking to her as a model of a woman who's made some hard choices about who she's going to be, despite what culture is telling her. Have you been hanging on to misconceptions about the Proverbs 31 woman?

PROVERBS 31 IS A POEM

Because it's a poem, Proverbs 31 should not be interpreted prescriptively as a job description for all women. Its purpose is to celebrate wisdom-in-action, not to instruct women everywhere to get married, have children, and take up the loom.

Ruth was called a woman of valour as a widow without children. Being a woman of valour means you can be single and be found in any season of life.

PROVERBS 31 IS WRITTEN FOR MEN AS ITS TARGET AUDIENCE

It's a Jewish tradition to read or sing Proverbs 31 at the beginning of Erev Shabbat on Friday nights in the Jewish household. Husbands sing it to their wives to honour them for making the house a home.

Proverbs 31 is *not* written to shame women into achieving every facet of this supposed to-do list. It is *not* written for women to try to "measure up." No one can be *all the things*! Rather, it's a *tribute* to every woman who is honouring God with her strong character, evident by the choices she makes day in and day out. Proverbs is for the *men* to study as a lesson in how to give tribute to the women in their lives.

PROVERBS 31 CELEBRATES VALOUR

The passage uses the same term, *eshet chayil*, to describe the virtuous woman as it uses to describe Ruth.

The late Rachel Held Evans reminds us of the following:

> Ruth was a destitute foreigner whose daily work involved gathering, threshing, and winnowing wheat. For most of her story, she is neither a wife nor a mother. Circumstantially, her life looked nothing like the life of the woman depicted in Proverbs 31.

Ruth didn't spend her days making clothes for her husband. She had no husband; she was widowed. Ruth's children didn't rise up and call her blessed. She was childless.

Ruth didn't spend her days exchanging fine linens with the merchants and keeping an immaculate home. She worked all day in the sun, gleaning leftovers from other people's fields, which was a provision made for the poorest of the poor in Israel. And yet guess what Boaz says of Ruth before she gets married, before she has a child, before she becomes a wealthy and influential woman: "All the people of my town know that you are a woman of noble character" *(Ruth 3:11)*. *The Hebrew that*'s used there is eshet chayil—woman of valor.[36]

Ruth is identified as a woman of valour not because she checked off some Proverbs 31 to-do list by getting married, keeping a clean house, and producing children, but because she lived her life with incredible bravery, wisdom, and strength. She lived her life with valour.

So how would *you* measure up to the Proverbs 31 woman on a scale of one to ten, now that you know her character was so much more than any "to-do" list? I hope it inspires you to look at your life right now and make some choices to step out in courage.

THE BRAVE TRUTH

Even when Ruth was "out," God had already provided a Kinsmen Redeemer for her to be brought "in." God is your Kinsmen Redeemer for your future, but you might have to wait to see it be fulfilled.

Ruth was part of the lineage of Christ. "*Salmon the father of Boaz, whose mother was Rahab, Boaz the father of Obed, whose mother was Ruth, Obed the father of Jesse, and Jesse the father of King David…*" (Matthew 1:5–6, NIV).

Remember to surrender yourself at Jesus' feet as an act of valour. He'll respond with an invitation to belonging and will act valiantly on your behalf for the rest of your life.

Courage is a matter of the heart.

Character is forged in the defining moments when a person must choose between right and right. Your identity is a matter of the heart. Ruth's identity, forged in fire, was so strong within her that it carried her above her culture, context, comfort, and need to conform.

Strength as a characteristic is important to God.

Elohim (or *Elohay*) is the first name for God found in the Bible, and it's used through the Old Testament over twenty-three hundred times. *Elohim* comes from the Hebrew root meaning "strength" or "power." *El Gibhor* (*Gibbor*) means the strong and mighty God. Combined with "El," it proclaims that *YHWH* (*Yahweh*) is the strong and mighty warrior God, as declared in Jeremiah 32:17–18:

> *Ah Lord YHWH! Behold, You have made the heavens and the earth by Your great power and by Your outstretched arm; there is nothing too hard for You, who show loving kindness to thousands, the great, the mighty God (El Gibhor), YHWH of Hosts is His name.* (World English Bible [WEB])

I think it's helpful to dig a bit deeper into the meanings of the words "gird" and "strength" to deepen our understanding of what it actually means to emulate the character trait of strength as women, like Ruth and the Proverbs 31 woman did.

Gird[37]:

- To put a belt, girdle, around the waist or hips
- To bind or secure with or as if with a belt—especially armour
- To surround; encircle
- To prepare oneself for action; to equip
- To endow with a rank in royalty or in an army

Strength[38]:

- The power to resist attack; impregnability
- The power to resist strain or stress; durability

- The ability to maintain a moral or intellectual position firmly
- Capacity or potential for effective action: a show of strength
- A source of power or force
- One that is regarded as the embodiment of protective or supportive power
- Degree of intensity, force, effectiveness, or potency in terms of a particular property
- Effective or binding force [I love this – what could we bind together with our strength?]

At what moments do you most need to be strong?

Despite Ruth's *external* reality of leaving behind everything she knew, moving to a foreign land as a woman who didn't fit in, what was Ruth's *internal* reality as a woman who became the very centre of the gospel story?

Ruth's "I Am…" statements might have been as follows:

- I Am… Complete
- I Am… Confident
- I Am… Resourceful
- I Am… Whole

If you were to complete "I Am…" statements, what would they be?

Valour isn't about what you *do*. It's about who you *are*.

The following verse is a stunning yet sobering reminder about why we're put on this earth—not just to survive, but to understand our place in God's bigger story and that we belong to Him. "*If we live, it's to honor the Lord. And if we die, it's to honor the Lord. So whether we live or die, we belong to Lord*" (Romans 14:8, NLT).

And we need to be reminded God has a particular place in His story for us to step in to, just as He did with Ruth in Matthew 1:5 and onwards… all the way down the royal line that leads to Jesus.

Where in the story would your name show up if God were writing it for you? You might be surprised to see how integral your brave choices were to creating and moving forward God's storyline of redemption and restoration.

If Scripture tells of a God who displays and elevates strength as a desirable character trait—along with depicting stories of women who choose to be strong—why, then, do we choose to live lives of defeat?

I have often used the chart below in coaching women who identify as victims in their circumstances, because they often don't realize the cost of living a weak vs. strong life.

In the first line, we can see the contrast between the strong life and the weak life and could draw a direct line to Ruth's choices. If Ruth had not been proactive in her situation upon finding herself a widow, she may have never left Moab, most likely remaining a single, and without a destiny. Instead, *she shaped her environment by being resourceful and making a choice to move forward into a new life.*

MY STRONG LIFE	MY WEAK LIFE
Self-managing, shapes environment, shows resourcefulness	Quickly offended, easily provoked, too sensitive, slow to recover
Responsive, intentional, thoughtful	Reactive, instinctive, automatic
Open, light-shedding, aware	Underhanded, covert, flourishes in the dark
Resilient, flexible, has a sense of proportion	Demanding, willful, stubborn, resistant (especially to reason and love), unbending
Have breadth of understanding, allow time for things to process	Think in black/white or yes/no, intolerant of ambiguity; seek final solution, want all or nothing
Take responsibility for self, learn when challenged, define self from within self	Blame, criticize, displace, fault-find, have poor discrimination
Relaxed, at ease, sensible	Uptight, serious, defensive
Take turns, collaborate, stay in touch even when tension grows	Competitive, either with or against, see life as contest, contemptuous
Clear, objective, purposeful	Vague, non-specific, cloaked
Create space, options, and common goals	Create too much or too little space and one sided solutions

Stop here and take some time to go through the above list to see where you can do some work in your own life to grow your character.

We all leave an emotional wake, positive or negative. Each of us owns the responsibility of ensuring our responses to difficult people and situations leave us resilient, keeping our options open. We don't have to complain. Nor do we need to be bitter. We don't have to close ourselves off if we've been hurt once. We don't have to blame someone else for our situation or believe we deserve better.

We often have more control over our choices than we think.

YOU CAN CHOOSE TO SHAPE YOUR ENVIRONMENT, BE RESOURCEFUL, AND MOVE FORWARD INTO A NEW LIFE.

Earlier, I shared that it was a difficult transition for me to move from my family of origin in Alberta to Ontario. About six months into my marriage, I was unhappy. I called home and talked to my mother about it. In true Ukrainian style, she asked if I had ever missed a meal. I replied I hadn't, so she declared, "You're staying!"

She was right. She saw through my unhappiness and discerned that the choice to settle and begin to create a home where happiness could flourish was a better one than coming home.

How about you? Do you find yourself in a place you never imagined you'd be? Have you ever felt like you've lost everything, even your identity? Be encouraged by Ruth's story and see what might be possible by being open to new options. Give things time to unfold. Most importantly, watch for God to honour your sweet obedience by providing solutions in the middle of your situation that you might never have thought of on your own.

Change is difficult. We like the status quo and try to hang on to what's comfortable. Sometimes we have the power to do that. But when change happens that's outside of our realm of control, we must remember we always have a choice in our response, even in a devastating loss. This is strength-building, character-forging grit.

Angela Duckworth, in her book, *Grit: The Power of Passion and Perseverance*, reminds us, "*When you keep searching for ways to change your situation for the better, you stand a chance of finding them. When you stop searching, assuming they can't be found, you guarantee they won't.*"[40]

Don't be scared of change. Don't be scared of living a strong life. Choose courage over culture, context, and the pressure to confirm. The world is waiting for you to live as a woman of valour—not trying harder, but finding your place in God's story, knowing who you are in your core. I believe there's so much room at the table for women who truly display the *eshet chayil* qualities. Would you step into your place in history and be that woman?

STUDY QUESTIONS

1. When have you ever felt "out?" How do you identify with Ruth at the beginning of her story?
2. When have you ever felt "in?" What did it feel like to belong? To be the right girl, the right family, the right culture, the right country, at the right time? What did you have to do to make that happen?
3. Read Hebrews 13:20–21. What makes you strong?
4. Read Ephesians 3:20–21. What makes you strong?
5. Read Matthew 28:18–20. What makes Jesus strong?
6. Are you identifying with the name *chayil*—woman of valour? How hard is it to live out valour right now, in your "before" story? How would you like to be remembered in your "after" story?
7. Read Psalm 84:5–7. Where do you start your journey and where will it end?

A MAKING BRAVE PRAYER

Lord, forgive me when I don't see myself as You do. Help me believe I was created to be named, like Ruth, *eshet chayil*, and that valour is not only about *what* I do, but, more importantly, *how* I do it.

When I feel "out" of the mainstream of Your plan, remind me that You graft those that are out, "in." Thank You that You are my Kinsmen Redeemer and have adopted me as Your Daughter. Thank You that the price You paid for my redemption is of the highest value because my Redeemer is Jesus Himself. Thank You that once you have adopted me, I will never be anything less than of the highest value to You.

I choose not to think like a woman who has no options. I choose to live my strong life, knowing that when I do, I'm becoming more and more like You. Thank You that all of my days are ordained for me and that my story, like Ruth's, is unique, and there's a future legacy that will come about because of my choices as a woman of valour.

I refuse to let my despair dictate my future outcomes. Thank You for being my Father, my Redeemer, my Friend. I love You, Lord. Amen.

EVEN WHEN THE PAST
CAN'T BE CHANGED,
THE FUTURE IS STILL
IN YOUR POWER.
DON'T GIVE IT AWAY.

7. A BRAVE RECOVERY–BATHSHEBA

Don't Give Away Your Power

Leave safety behind. Put your body on the line. Stand before the people you fear and speak your mind—even if your voice shakes. When you least expect it, someone may actually listen to what you have to say. Well-aimed slingshots can topple giants. And do your homework.

—Maggie Kuhn[41]

KALLIE'S STORY:

My name is Kallie Wood, or in Cree, nawmahach ota' ochoa asisky, which translates to "not of this earth."

"Bravery is to face the foe with integrity and courage"— an excerpt included in our First Nation Seven Sacred Teachings. I am a resilient Nakoda Cree First Nation woman from Treaty Four Territory in Saskatchewan, Canada; a daughter, sister, aunt, mother, and kokum, who today, has her feet planted firmly on Mother Earth… but the journey to get here has not been easy and here's why.

A complex journey since birth, full of loss of family, culture, language, and identity—not by choice but rather by forced circumstance—has shaped me into a stranger in my own story. It leaves a girl with only two options: fight or flight. I choose to fight, to be brave! My "a-ha!" moment occurred when an Elder shared with me, "spread your wings or you will have no idea how far you can fly." Spread my wings I did, reconnecting to my First Nation identity and today sharing my story around the globe to educate and open paths of reconciliation and inspiration for a better tomorrow for our children and grandchildren.

It's not easy leading bravely in our own stories, but man, when we do, we take the power back to write our own endings. I choose brave and I don't let people pull me into their storm, I pull them into my peace.[42]

Meryl Streep, Steve Martin, and Alec Baldwin starred in the 2009 movie, *It's Complicated*. Streep's character had been divorced from Baldwin's character for years. When she became interested in Martin's character, her ex-husband showed up and lured her back into a relationship. How would you describe that situation? It's complicated!

Looking at the story of David and Bathsheba, I'd bet no two people would agree on who was responsible for how she ended up in his palace, in his bed—a married woman whose husband was one of David's key warriors.

We often find ourselves in situations, such as a relationship breakdown, in which we want to blame someone or lay the responsibility at someone's feet, based on the credibility of one person or the other. It becomes a matter of he said/she said. We don't like it when things aren't settled and there's no one to blame. We like to clarify who was right and who was wrong.

But in the story of David and Bathsheba, *it's complicated*.

Maybe things are "complicated" and confusing for you too. And this can stop you from being brave, as you wonder if you're a victim or victor. You either carry shame for something that wasn't your fault or deflect responsibility for something you need to own up to.

Where did Bathsheba's bravery get her?

Bathsheba is probably one of the most controversial and misunderstood women who ever lived. She has been labelled both a victim and a vixen. But her story is important because, just like women before her, she was chosen to be a significant player in the lineage of Jesus.

Bathsheba had to find a way to overcome her complicated circumstances. She had to be bigger than what she suffered. *We* have to be bigger than the things we suffer.

So who was this woman? She's mostly known for bathing on the roof, catching King David's attention, and committing adultery with him. She's a figure associated with shame, known as one who caused the king's downfall. At best, she's a victim of circumstances, a consenting weak woman who had not resisted an obvious sin; at worst, she's a shameless, adulterous woman who schemed her way into the high places of the royal palace.

Yet God had chosen this controversial woman to bring forth the lineage of Christ. Both the earthly father and mother of Jesus—Joseph and Mary—were her direct descendants. The Scriptures say that Bathsheba bore four sons to King David: Solomon, Nathan, Shimea, and Shobab and among them, two were direct forefathers of Jesus. Joseph, Mary's husband, came from the lineage of Solomon (Matthew 1:6) and Mary, Joseph's wife, was a direct descendant of Nathan (Luke 3:31).

She carried within her veins the blood of spiritual royalty.

God makes no mistakes in honouring whom He chooses, even the least likely. Bathsheba's firstborn son, Solomon, was chosen to be the first successor to King David.

Why would God choose to honour this woman throughout the history of His holy nation Israel, where so much emphasis is placed on genealogical uprightness? He chooses whom He will choose. And you should know by now that there's a place for *you* in God's story!

There were many other sons borne to David's other wives, sons who were not tainted with such a bad reputation and as misunderstood. Yet God picked this "woman of shame" to bring forth the successor.

Let's take a look at why Bathsheba was so honoured by God.

Her complicated love story with David began in 2 Samuel 11:2–4:

One evening David got up from his bed and walked around on the roof of the palace. From the roof he saw a woman bathing. The woman was very beautiful, and David sent someone to find out about her. The man said, "She is Bathsheba, the daughter of Eliam and the wife of Uriah the Hittite." Then David sent messengers to get her. She came to him, and he slept with her. (Now she was purifying herself from her monthly uncleanness.) Then she went back home. (NIV)

Readers might assume Bathsheba lacked modesty since she was bathing in the open, or in a place open enough for the king to see her clearly from his palace. They assume she must've carefully timed the hour when the king would be taking his evening walk on the rooftop of his palace. And she must've moved her naked body seductively to seize David's attention when he was vulnerable, after his afternoon nap.

Or did she?

A closer look at Scripture reveals a different picture. First, it was customary of women in those days to bathe and do their washings at the wells; they did so in the evening, just before dusk set in, when it was cooler and darker.

Second, the Bible does not say that Bathsheba was bathing in the open. She was the granddaughter of Ahithophel, a high-powered advisor to King David, whose advice was treated as the oracles of God. Her husband, Uriah, was a commander and armour bearer to the chief commander, Joab, so the family likely had a private well within the compound. Bathsheba was bathing in her own enclosed courtyard, which was private and legitimate. She wasn't doing anything out of the ordinary for the custom and culture of her time.

Third, Scripture doesn't even state that she was naked. She could very well have bathed with a cloth wrapped around her.

Fourth, she couldn't have known whether King David was in the palace or taking an evening walk on the rooftop. She was a commoner; it was neither her privilege nor her business to know about the King's schedule.

The presumption that she was a "loose woman" and seductress is unsubstantiated. Has Bathsheba been misjudged through all these generations? Do we *still* misjudge her?

DAVID'S SIDE OF THE STORY

David had experienced an unprecedented period of success, both personally and politically. He was idle, with little to do but relax and enjoy his position as king, able to do most anything he wanted and have anything he desired. He had already violated God's law in multiplying wives and concubines (Deuteronomy 17:17).

"No temptation has overtaken you except what is common to mankind. And God is faithful; he will not let you be tempted beyond what you can bear. But when you are tempted, he will also provide a way out so that you can endure it"

—I Corinthians 10:13, NIV

Was this true for David, or did he manage to turn off his conscience so he could go after what he wanted?

BATHSHEBA'S SIDE OF THE STORY

Scripture isn't clear on whether Bathsheba resisted when David sent for Bathsheba. Did she consent, or did she fear his power? I believe the latter. David likely didn't make his true intentions known until it was too late. Bathsheba was dealing with the warrior who had subdued even powerful armies and succeeded in all of his endeavours. She couldn't just say "no."

This scenario resonates with the #MeToo movement sweeping the globe. Women who have been victimized are rising up to tell their stories of sexual harassment and assault, describing feelings of helplessness and having no choice, no other options.

What were Bathsheba's options? There was a rule in the Talmud, the Jewish oral law, that stated Bathsheba could've delivered herself out of this situation of shame and sin by quickly divorcing Uriah, who wouldn't come to her, despite the king's order, because of his faithfulness to serving the king. She could then demand that David take her as his wife, since she was pregnant.

But Bathsheba didn't do any of that. She chose not to divorce Uriah, leaving her fate in the hands of her king and her God, and being found guilty of the sin of adultery. She became known throughout history as the woman who had caused King David's downfall.

Why didn't she renounce her husband and save herself? Was she indeed a virtuous woman and faithful wife with character, forced to choose one right over another?

When Bathsheba discovered her pregnancy with David's child, David tried to fool Uriah into believing the child was his. An already-complicated situation full of secrets became darker as the story progressed, as ultimately, David felt his only option was to have Uriah murdered.

Raped, pregnant, and now having lost her husband—all at the hands of the king—Bathsheba held little power to change the situation. She would've felt used and betrayed, and could've turned bitter. But she didn't try and deliver herself by her own means. She stood alone, waiting, leaving her destiny in God's hands. She lived her faith. Later, she lifted up her countenance in dignity as the wife of the king, even in the face of public criticism. She paid a high price for someone else's actions—her child died. Yet God expressed His displeasure with and judgment against *David*, never Bathsheba.

David ultimately respected and favoured Bathsheba, spiritually and as a companion. Their love lasted a lifetime.

In the end, on the advice of the prophet Nathan, Bathsheba went to David to ensure Solomon's place on the throne, despite complicated "sister-wives" vying for their sons to take it instead.

She continued in bravery to become an honoured Queen Mother.

When Bathsheba went to King Solomon to speak to him for Adonijah, the king stood up to meet her, bowed down to her and sat down on his throne. He had a throne brought for the king's mother, and she sat down at his right hand.

—1 Kings 2:19, NIV

No Queen Mother mentioned in the Bible was treated with as much honour and respect as Bathsheba. The wisest man who ever lived (Solomon) knew that others would look at her as a figure of shame, but he chose to uphold his mother with unsurpassed respect. His respect and vindication of her is a testimony to the kind of life Bathsheba led.

What lessons can we learn from Bathsheba's life? She enjoyed the complicity of success. But she was susceptible when she:

- let down her defences
- left herself exposed
- let in temptation

She trusted when she shouldn't have trusted and let down her defences. Things got complicated from here.

But Bathsheba has shown us how to make the best choices possible in a complicated situation, either as a victim or collaborator. Even though it was complicated and we're not quite sure of her involvement, there was brave work Bathsheba had to do. And she did the work.

A PERSON TO FORGIVE

"And when you stand praying, if you hold anything against anyone, forgive them, so that your Father in heaven may forgive you your sins" (Mark 11:25, NIV). Bathsheba would have had to forgive David to prevent carrying around the bitterness of what he had allowed in her life.

A PAST TO FORGET

> *Yet if you devote your heart to him and stretch out your hands to him, if you put away the sin that is in your hand and allow no evil to dwell in your tent, then, free of fault, you will lift up your face; you will stand firm and without fear.*
>
> *You will surely forget your trouble, recalling it only as waters gone by.*
>
> —Job 11:13–16, NIV

Bathsheba had to forget the past so she could stand tall, free of fault and free of fear, looking towards her future.

A FUTURE TO FOCUS ON

Philippians 3:13–14 says, *"Forgetting what is behind and straining toward what is ahead, I press on toward the goal to win the prize for which God has called me heavenward in Christ Jesus"* (NIV). As Bathsheba looked towards the future, she saw Solomon and she saw legacy.

What are the lessons from David's life? He had to understand these things in order to move forward in His life, in His relationship with Bathsheba, and for the sake of future generations.

THERE IS A CONSEQUENCE FOR SIN

"After the time of mourning was over, David had her brought to his house, and she became his wife and bore him a son. But the thing David had done displeased the Lord."

—2 Samuel 11:27, NIV

THERE IS A CONFESSION FOR SIN

"Have mercy on me, O God, according to your unfailing love; according to your great compassion blot out my transgressions. Wash away all my iniquity and cleanse me from my sin."

—Psalm 51:1–2, NIV

THERE IS A COVERING FOR SIN

"Then David comforted his wife Bathsheba, and he went to her and made love to her. She gave birth to a son, and they named him Solomon. The Lord loved him."

—2 Samuel 12:24, NIV

"If you, Lord, kept a record of sins, Lord, who could stand? But with you there is forgiveness, so that we can, with reverence, serve you"

—Psalm 130:3–4

THE BRAVE TRUTH

David's instruction to Solomon showed that maybe he had learned the lesson of sin's consequences and wanted to spare Solomon from making the same mistakes he did.

Observe what the Lord your God requires: Walk in obedience to him, and keep his decrees and commands, his laws and regulations, as written in the Law of Moses. Do this so that you may prosper in all you do and wherever you go.

—1 Kings 2:3, NIV

Here are principles and Scriptures that promise blessing, even out of the most challenging circumstances, if we determine to be obedient"

- You will be fruitful in the land of your affliction. (Isaiah 61:1–3)
- When you walk through the fire you will not be scorched. (Isaiah 43:2–4)
- A weapon of destruction can be a tool of construction in your life. (Isaiah 61:4)
- What is ahead of you is so much more important than what is behind you.
- Do not become content with the complacency that comes with success.
- Focus on moving from success to significance

BATHSHEBA'S BRAVE MOMENT

For the sake of the royal lineage of Jesus, it was necessary for Bathsheba to not only own her place in the story, but also encourage David to be the man who would act like a true king. The future was at stake! This lineage connected Rahab, Ruth, and Bathsheba:

Salmon the father of Boaz, whose mother was Rahab,
Boaz the father of Obed, whose mother was Ruth,
Obed the father of Jesse, and Jesse the father of King David. David was the father of Solomon, whose mother had been Uriah's wife.

—Matthew 1:5–6, NIV

"What is it you want?" the king asked. [Bathsheba] said to him, "My lord, you yourself swore to me your servant by the Lord your God: 'Solomon your son shall be king after me, and he will sit on my throne.'"
—1 Kings 1:16–17, NIV

I love my friend Kallie's words from the beginning of this chapter: *"It's not easy leading bravely in our own stories, but man, when we do, we take the power back to write our own endings."*

When Bathsheba understood that she held power with David, she didn't shy away from the consequences of speaking out truth. She demanded that David honour his promise that her son (Solomon) would carry on as king after David. This was bravery at its finest.

Despite the complexity of Bathsheba's life, and finding herself complicit in a story she didn't create, she found her power and wrote her own ending, as well as the beginning of the story that would come after her.

When Solomon wrote the Book of Proverbs, Bathsheba was his influence for writing the famous Chapter 31 because he knew she was a virtuous woman, despite her complicated beginning with David. There can be much pain in relationships between men and women, especially when you're forced to be with someone you never chose.

But if Bathsheba can find a brave ending to her story, it opens up possibilities for us to find our brave in circumstances that are extreme, clouded with gray. Would you be brave enough not to conform as you feel you should at times, but step out and speak truth to power for the sake of future generations, as Bathsheba did? I believe in your courage to do this very thing. Don't give away your power. Use it to speak truth for the sake of the future.

STUDY QUESTIONS

1. If you've been a victim of someone else's choices, how does Bathsheba's story encourage you?
2. How susceptible are you to sin?
3. Where can you become complacent in your success?
4. What are some ways you can move yourself from success to significance?

A MAKING BRAVE PRAYER

Father, forgive me for the times I've put myself in a situation in which I've been susceptible to sin. Guard my ways and only let me walk in paths that do not cast doubt on my character. Give me the wisdom to not be complicit in someone else's wrong choices. If I've been wronged, please give me the courage to speak truth to power.

I rely on Your wisdom and Your protection. Thank You for raising me up and allowing me to be part of Your bigger story. Amen.

THE MORE WE LET
GOD TAKE US OVER,
THE MORE TRULY
OURSELVES WE BECOME.

8. A BRAVE SURRENDER—MARY

Don't Worry About What Everyone Else Thinks

God wants us to learn how to accept every unexpected event as an invitation to trust Him.

—Christine Caine[43]

BONNIE'S STORY:

In spring 2018, my husband and I sat down with our lead pastors, Mitch and Bonnie, for a conversation. We could all sense a big change was coming. They asked us, "If you could do anything in the world, what would you do?"

My husband and I had been serving in a leadership role with our home church, HillCity Church, in Abbotsford, B.C., for our entire adult lives. Youth ministry. Children's ministry. Young adult ministry. Men and women. We were committed to serving the vision of our home church.

But something new and unique was stirring in us—and had been for many years.

Early on in our Christian lives, we had both been gripped by the sorrow and ramifications we could see in our generation because of negative sexual experiences and confusion about identities. Over time, we had begun to pray more and more that God would release us to be an influence to bring healing and hope to people around the world.

While we were raising our five young sons, homeschooling, and my husband working a job in trades, we would squeeze things into our schedule that matched this dream. I wrote blog articles, we hosted events to bring a message of truth, and we met with and counselled young people. We would crawl into bed well past midnight on many occasions, sometimes crying over the heartache that someone had shared with us, sometimes celebrating over their breakthrough and victory.

The reality is that when we scratch the surface, issues around sexuality and relationships has affected us all in a variety of ways.

So when our pastors asked us this bold question, it wasn't long before we found words to answer. "We want to bring a message of truth and hope about God's design for sexuality, and empower other voices to talk about how God has restored them."

Over time, we formulated the plan for a ministry called "The Union." We became full-time missionaries, with a home base in North America, financially supported by the generosity of those who saw the value in a movement like this.

Many people were shocked at this choice. They were happy for us, but then they would say, "I could never do that."

Others have bluntly asked, "How can you afford to live?" They would look us in the eye, looking for hints of fear.

And waves of intimidation have certainly come, trying to knock us off of our feet. But, early on in the process of development, my husband and I had a conversation about it. We both agreed that as scary as it can be to step out for the sake of a dream, what scares us far more is the thought of letting life pass us by, unwilling to take a risk. Safe, but not fulfilled.

I'd have much greater regret in being contained by fear than in bravely inching our way forward in the direction that we feel the Father leading us.[44]

Mary was a woman admired for her bravery and loved for her devotion to God. She walked a difficult path, knowing how costly her submission would be. The virgin birth of her Son, Jesus, defied scientific logic. Mary is recognized most as the mother to God's only Son. This is the "now" story for which we already know the outcome.

If we transport ourselves right back into Mary's life in *her* "now" story, so much of what we understand as common knowledge about the birth of Christ and what it has meant for our salvation is information Mary couldn't fully grasp then. The admiration of Mary that we have now because of her brave surrender to God's will in her life is not something she experienced in her lifetime.

Where did Mary's bravery get her?

As in Bonnie's story, when you make a decision to say "yes" to God, it might not be applauded or understood by the people around you.

God chose Mary for what could be arguably the most important job in history—bringing Christ into the world. She was the perfect unlikely choice, which made her story even more remarkable.

Whom does God choose to participate in His plan? As we've seen throughout this book, He often favours women whom most would say would be unlikely candidates for greatness or extraordinary destiny. From Eve, who made her worst choice on her worst day, to Sarah, who gave birth well beyond her prime, to Leah, who was unloved by her husband but beloved by God, to Jochebed, a Hebrew mother who broke the law to save her son, to Rahab the prostitute, to Ruth the foreigner, to Bathsheba the victim... all the way to Mary, the young, single, innocent girl. Together, they form a hall of fame of "she-saints" in the Bible.

This brave lineup stamps on our hearts the incredulous possibility that God can use you and me if He chooses. Even if you are the least likely. Even if you are unproven and had never had a brave moment in your life up until now. Even if your knees are shaking but you are sensing this is the moment He's whispering an invitation to you to choose courage now. If He chooses to invite you to step into something you would never have dreamed for yourself, you always have a choice to say "yes." Or "no."

What we often forget is that we have a choice in how to respond.

We venerate Mary for her surrender to the will of God when she responds so humbly to the angel. "*I am the Lord's servant,' Mary answered. 'May your word to me be fulfilled'*" (Luke 1:38, NIV).

These are some of the greatest words any woman has ever spoken.

But if we back up in her story, this is the end of the conversation, not the beginning. The conversation that came before is found in Luke 1:28–37:

The angel went to her and said, "Greetings, you who are highly fa-
vored! The Lord is with you." Mary was greatly troubled at his words
and wondered what kind of greeting this might be. But the angel said
to her, "Do not be afraid, Mary; you have found favor with God. You
will conceive and give birth to a son, and you are to call him Jesus. He
will be great and will be called the Son of the Most High. The Lord
God will give him the throne of his father David, and he will reign
over Jacob's descendants forever; his kingdom will never end."

"How will this be," Mary asked the angel, "since I am a virgin?"
The angel answered, "The Holy Spirit will come on you, and the power
of the Most High will overshadow you. So the holy one to be born will
be called the Son of God. Even Elizabeth your relative is going to have
her old age, and she who was said to be unable to conceive is in her
sixth month. For no word from God will ever fail." (NIV)

I've often wondered, when Mary agreed to the angel's words, whether it
was the last step in a series of moments of wrestling that went on inside of her.

If we sense a call in our lives to be the brave woman and make a bold
move, how do we feel in the moment when the time comes, and the voice of
God comes to us clearly (even if faintly)?

Consider the following three stages of our reactions that we need to
process before we respond.

WE DON'T BELIEVE THE MESSENGER

The Greek word used for "greatly troubled" is *diatarasso, an intensified ver-*
sion of the verb tarasso. This verb literally means "stirred," "mixed," or "jum-
bled up," and from that root the word also can come to mean "troubled" *or*
"agitated." Closer to the root meaning, however, is the idea that this mental
stirring or mixing means "confused."

When the messenger comes, we aren't sure it's God's voice. It might
be because we aren't familiar enough with His voice, which causes us to
doubt it's really Him. Mary knew the Scriptures, but perhaps hadn't taken
to heart the stories of God's call coming to women before her.

We tend to be fearful of anything we don't understand. I suggest the antidote is to get to know the God of the Bible by studying the stories and trying to understand how He speaks to His people. It's a shock when He speaks, because He challenges our understanding. When He comes to us in a still, small voice, or when His words leap off the pages of Scripture and we know they were meant for us personally, the experience "messes" with us a bit. God doesn't intend for us to remain the same after any interaction with His Word. His message is meant to turn our lives upside down, to radically transform us from the inside out, to challenge our traditions and beliefs, and look at Him for *who He is*, not whom we have made Him to be.

No wonder the message can be confusing, troubling, and even leave us a bit shaken. He wants to rock us out of our world and jettison us into His bold mission.

He often speaks to us when we least expect it.

The desire to launch Gather Women was planted in my heart at a season in life when my response was, "Really, God, now? It's so inconvenient!" It usually is. But you can't wait to say "yes" until you have the perfect marriage, the perfect job, the perfect ministry, the perfect anything. He doesn't usually find you there. He finds you when you're busy minding your own business, keeping your head low, and trying not to be noticed. And that's why it's such a shock to be called into action.

We might lie in bed at night, dreaming of doing big things for God. But we never imagine they'll ever happen. And guess what? Never say never. If it happened to Mary, it can happen to you. Are you humble enough to be open to the message of supernatural mobilization when it comes? Will you accept it full on, no matter what it takes?

WE DON'T BELIEVE THE MESSAGE

To have a message spoken to you about something you'd never dream or imagine in your life time would be a shock. To have a message spoken to you about the fact that your body would be impregnated by the Holy Spirit and you would be the vehicle for delivering the Saviour of the universe would be beyond anyone's comprehension. Mary's reaction would be so justified. Can this really be true? Is it beyond belief?

When God calls you to step out in brave faith to something you'd never dreamed or imagined, you might also not quite believe it. But you need to wrap your head around the fact that from this point on, everything will change. Nothing will be the same.

Much of the time, we're not ready to let go of our preconceived plan of what our life will look like. We need to let go of the deep attachments we have to our life, our possessions, and our dreams. Thomas Merton calls these "secret attachments." To uproot these, he cautions that "we need to leave the initiative in the hands of God working in our souls either directly in the night of aridity and suffering, or through events and other men."[45]

If it doesn't fit your idea of the fairy-tale ending, or mesh with your five-year or retirement plan, you don't believe it can be true. If it doesn't increase your platform or heal your cancer, you can't believe God would be asking you to do this thing.

Can you suspend your idea of what you think the message will be and instead have an open heart and open ears to hear it when it comes?

WE DON'T BELIEVE THE MESSAGE IS MEANT FOR US

Mary was young. She was single—betrothed, but single. And this message was scandalous. She would never choose herself or her womb to carry the Son of God. She was likely incredulous that God would choose her. I believe it was her humility that God had seen that made her the perfect woman for the role.

When God's calling us, do we think more about how this would radically change and disrupt every plan we were making? Mary was making wedding plans, and we're busy making vacation plans, ministry plans, birthday celebration plans, all kinds of plans in our ordinary lives. Then God comes along and flips everything to His heavenly agenda. Nothing will ever be the same. How does He know if our hearts will be humble enough in the moment to choose His plans over our agendas?

What Mary was truly saying to the angel was "yes" to a radical disruption of life as she knew it. She was saying "yes" to a radical disruption of her reputation as she knew it. She was saying "yes" to allowing someone—God's Son—to grow within her. She was saying "yes" to a new identity. She had no idea that we would be reading her story today and learning from her humble and surrendered "yes."

"Let it be to me according to your word" (Luke 1:38). Those were the words Mary spoke to the angel when he announced to her that she would give birth to God's Son, the words that ushered her into the gestation of divinity and the experience of waiting. With them, she let go of her own will and the security of her old way of life and instead yielded to God's purposes.

Have you ever stepped out in total obedience to God with those around you, not understanding why, and then waited for years to have your calling "proved?"

Years ago, I believed I had come to the end of my time serving in worship and performance. I had given my best and had experienced some amazing times of worship and creativity. But I thought I was done, and that God's desire was to put me on the shelf for a season.

In the middle of that time, I was invited to a gathering of leaders to discuss a weeklong revival in Toronto, with plans to bring in various Christian speakers from around the world. I remember feeling like I didn't belong there, but I went because a dear friend had invited me. There was a short promo video played of Anne Graham Lotz inviting listeners to join an upcoming "Just Give Me Jesus" revival.

Anne had done over 20 of these revivals in large arenas all over the world, and this was now a consideration for Toronto. I was so moved while the promo video played, and I knew I was called to, at the very least, lick envelopes for the mailings that would go out and invite people to attend. I honestly believed that my contribution would take place tucked away in a back office, unseen.

As it turned out, all the leaders abandoned the planned revival week and the call came to *me* to serve as the "Just Give Me Jesus" revival co-chair for Toronto, working with Anne Graham Lotz.

During this time, I resonated with Mary's heart as she wondered how and why God would ask her to be the mother of the Saviour of the world. He was asking me to take on this enormous task for my city of three million, and as I felt the pressing of the call on my heart, I was also looking around and wondering where all the other women were—women God could have chosen, women who might've been much better choices.

Even my church small group, in response to my announcement that I was called to step out and lead the revival, responded initially with, *"You?"*

I, like Mary, didn't believe the messenger. I thought my heart and my mind were playing tricks with me, or that I was proud and deluded to think I could lead any initiative of this magnitude.

I, like Mary, didn't believe the message. I had only known the world of creative arts, and this was largely a ministry to women, something I had shied away from most of my life. This was way out of my area of expertise.

I, like Mary, didn't believe the message was for me. I had forgotten that not long before, at a leadership training weekend for women, God had given me a vision entirely out of context. We were given blank paper and asked to sketch a vision for our lives. I was in my "on-the-shelf" season and didn't believe I had anything to offer. But as I sat and contemplated, I began to draw.

What appeared on the paper were stick figure images of women coming in twos and threes, with broken hearts, to a curtain. As they approached the veil-like draping, it was pulled open. As they stood and watched in wonder, the face of Christ was revealed behind the veil, not as they had believed Him to be (in my mind I had thought He was never pleased with me), but looking at them, full of love in His eyes. As they stood there, Christ reached out His hand to each of them, mended their broken hearts, and wrote a new name on their forehead.

I had not felt the favour of God on my life and discounted myself from being called to participate in something so magnificent. But I remembered He had healed my heart and called me to be the woman He created me to be and accept the name He had written on my forehead.

I had a choice to say "yes" or "no." And once my "yes" was spoken, I could no longer worry about what anyone would think about me being a suitable choice for this leadership role.

I know that Mary's "yes" to the angel was solid and true, based on total submission to God. I wonder if she truly knew the scope of all she was saying "yes" to. I know I had no idea that the two years of full-time ministry to prepare to invite thousands of men and women to the Air Canada Centre in Toronto would cost me in ways I could never imagine. The faithful team of women raised to work together on the revival also experienced significant challenges in their lives. We prayed our way through, but when the doors of the arena opened on September 29, 2006, we had no idea what the outcome would be.

I sat in the arena at the end of that evening when Anne Graham Lotz gave the invitation to come to the cross and meet Jesus. She had a rough-hewn cross on the platform to stand as the symbol of Christ's sacrifice. When she gave the invitation, it was like the arena emptied in a "whoosh" as men and women left their seats and came to the cross in hordes—the Bride of Christ coming to the Bridegroom.

In that moment, I felt God's favour on my life like I'd never experienced it. He was holding me so close to His beating heart. I witnessed thousands coming to the cross, exchanging their shame for His glory and going on to complete hundreds of Bible studies across the province and beyond. I couldn't believe I had been allowed the privilege of participating in this supernatural moving of God.

Mary understood the magnitude of her decision to say "yes" when God chose her. Her knowledge of God's promise to send a Saviour for His people showed through her worship. And then she settled into a life of being Jesus' mother and maybe felt that she was solely responsible for His upbringing and future. She might've thought she had some measure of control over Him as His mother, and maybe for a while, He obeyed.

We are so used to asking God to answer our prayers in the way *we* would answer our own prayers if *we* were God. But He doesn't.

Mary found this out when she approached Jesus at the wedding of Cana when the wine had run out. She had been waiting all her life for proof that her "yes" to the angel and to God had not been in vain.

I wonder if Mary had been ridiculed for thirty years leading up to this moment because of her perceived promiscuity and because of how many people believed that Joseph was not the father of Jesus. Nothing had been proven one way or another, because the Scriptures telling the whole story of Jesus had not yet come to reality. We know the whole story now, but Mary, as much as she believed she was participating in the greater purposes of God, had still to see the full result of her "yes."

If He was truly Jesus, why hadn't he done anything yet to prove His divinity?

At the wedding of Cana, Mary seized an opportunity to take things into her own hands and settle the rumours, once and for all. Here, in public, Jesus could prove Himself, and she would be vindicated.

So she approached Jesus at the wedding and said plainly, "They have no wine."

This is much like what I would say to my husband, Stephen, if we were entertaining and ran out of ice: "We have no ice." What I really mean is, "Stephen, please get in the car and go get us some ice!" I don't say it, but I mean it.

Mary didn't ask Jesus for more wine. She made a statement. She knew that culturally, a rabbi usually started his earthly ministry at the age of thirty, Jesus' age. Here was his opportunity. In her mind, it was "go time."

"Jesus' mother told Jesus, 'They have no wine,' and Jesus replied, 'Woman, what has this to do with me? My hour has not yet come'" (John 2:3–4, ESV).

I believe Mary was asking for more of what they already had. In her expectation of Jesus' response, she was thinking He could simply get more wine.

But Jesus was not that easily persuaded. He explained it wasn't His time and called her "Woman" instead of "Mother." He wasn't being rude; his response was culturally acceptable, but He was sending two strong messages to Mary—two theological truths on which He would base His earthly ministry:

1. *Jesus was putting appropriate distance between Himself and His mother and her authority.* Reality changed, literally in an instant, because He became focused on doing the Father's work. As an adult, He wasn't obligated to obey His mother. He made clear that there was a higher authority in His life.

2. *Jesus was pushing back against the suggestion that He was responsible for getting more of what others already had.* He knew that what He would offer them was something they couldn't get more of themselves. He was offering them "new wine," something so unique and supernatural, that it would be evident that it was transformational and miraculous.

THE BRAVE TRUTH

We presume much when we pray and ask God to meet our needs. We presume that His primary concern is to cater to what *we* think the best solution would be. We pray "safe" prayers, not prayers of brave women. We think, like Mary did, that we have waited too long to be vindicated, and it's time for Him to set things right. We're "good" for asking Him for more. We want more possessions, more influence, more followers, more friends, more of what we've run out of.

But Jesus wants to give us something *new*—not more of what we have. Brave prayers pull out all the stops and ask for supernatural transformation and a way of living that can be accessed only through the power of the Holy Spirit.

Jesus is not in the business of giving us old wine.

In order to receive the new wine, we must have new wineskins. We must be able to carry, through more faith and capacity, all that He wants to pour into our lives. He wants to pour greater faith and fruit, and prepare us for a greater future than we could ever imagine for ourselves.

Mary's brave "yes" gave her entrance into the significant role of raising the Saviour. Your brave "yes" gives you entrance into the significant role of influencing generations coming behind you that you have no idea will read of your "yes," and be encouraged in their response to God.

Don't worry about what everyone else thinks about your "yes." It's not worth it. Jesus wasn't worried what Mary would think when He clearly stated He was here to do the work of the Father. Do you and I believe we are placed here for the same reason? Say "yes!"

Your brave is now.

STUDY QUESTIONS

1. In all her humanity, amid all her fears, doubts, and worries, Mary was a woman who said "yes" to God—no matter the risk or price that it would eventually cost her. Do you walk with such intimacy with Him that His voice is made clear amid the confusion of your circumstances?

2. Read Luke 1:45: *"Blessed is she who has believed that the Lord would fulfill his promises to her!"* (NIV). What does it mean to believe? For followers of Jesus, is there room for doubt in the midst of faith?

3. We can't speculate regarding what Mary believed about Jesus' resurrection before He died. But whether she was confident or uncertain, we know she was present during His crucifixion, and we can imagine that it was absolutely heart-wrenching for her to watch. If we have faith that God will make all things new (Revelations 21:5) and that all things work together for good (Romans 8:28), does that affect our "at-the-cross" experiences? If so, how? If not, why not?

4. Mary experienced the miraculous through a prophetic encounter, an angel appearance, and the virgin birth, but we have no reason *not* to believe that for the majority of her life, she experienced God in the midst of ordinary, everyday life. For example, it's no coincidence that she turned to Jesus at an ordinary wedding when they ran out of wine, looking to Him to fill the need. Does God still desire to display his supernatural power in ordinary settings? Have you ever seen or experienced this?

5. Think about the last time you were scared to death to do something you knew you were supposed to do, but did it anyway. What was the result?

6. Name the doubts, fears, and anxieties you feel when you think about the "scary yes." Again, write them down. Take some time to reflect and pray over what you know God's asking you to say "yes" to.

A MAKING BRAVE PRAYER

Father, please keep me humble in my posture when You call me to something so extraordinary that I can't fathom that I would be the woman You chose. Help me to push through the confusion, fear, and doubt, and get to my "yes" at the right time. Help me see beyond what people think of me or my reputation in my "yes" moment.

Help me envision the future You've planned and how significant my response is to the building of Your kingdom. Help me believe that future generations will be encouraged by my "yes." I pray they will be emboldened for Your sake, and for the glory of Your name and Your name alone. Amen.

 CONFIDENCE ONLY TAKES YOU SO FAR. YOU WILL NEED RADICAL CONVICTION TO FINISH STRONG.

9. A BRAVE ENDING—BRING BRAVE HOME

Don't Ever Quit

Regardless of what came before, or what is yet to come, what matters most right now is how I choose to respond to the challenge before me. Will I lie down or will I fight? The choice is mine, and I choose to finish strong.

—Dan Green[46]

WHERE WILL YOUR BRAVERY GET YOU?

In every brave life, there's a beginning, a middle, and an end. Each is a season all to its own, and each must end before a new one can begin. If you start at the beginning of life, you're reminded that all life began in a garden—and it was stunning.

When the first woman who ever lived (Eve) took her first breath, she was called into a life that had an accepting, an appointing, and an anointing. It was life as it was meant to be lived in all its beauty because it included an *unbroken relationship with God*. It was perfection before shame-making, barrier-creating sin got in the way through one act of disobedience.

Eve was designed for purpose, and so were you. Eve fully belonged in the world God created her for. Eve was appointed to do good work alongside Adam, ruling over the animals and creation. Eve was anointed with birthright gifts to do the work only *she* could do. She was unique in every way.

Eve was *ezer kenegdo*.

Ezer - this is the Hebrew word which is translated "helper" and is used by hierarchalists to infer a position of subordination for Eve (the helper) and thus for all women and consequently a position of authority for Adam (the one being helped) and thus for all men. The frequent use, however, in the OT to refer to God negates any meaning of subordination and the fact that ezer is modified by kenegdo meaning "face to face" or "equivalent to" rules out any idea of superiority on the part of this human helper.[47]

So are you.

You and I live in the "broken middle." The beginning was full of so much potential for both man and woman—a never-ending dance with the Trinity while carrying out the purpose-filled life for which they were created. That was the beginning, but this is now. The beginning had no barrier between God and man—until it was broken. We would still be in our "broken" now, with no hope, if Jesus hadn't come and laid down His life as the bridge to create the way to a new beginning.

David had a sense of the larger narrative arc of God's story. He reached back into the beginning and captured some of the destiny that was meant for you in God's original, loving design.

Psalm 139:13–16:

For you created my inmost being;
you knit me together in my mother's womb.
I praise you because I am fearfully and wonderfully made;
your works are wonderful,
I know that full well.
My frame was not hidden from you
when I was made in the secret place,
when I was woven together in the depths of the earth.
Your eyes saw my unformed body;
all the days ordained for me were written in your book
before one of them came to be. (NIV)

Even though you're in the "broken middle," Jesus made it possible to live the life you were created to live. To truly grasp these words, you should be full of wonder at the beauty and complexity of God's creation, which includes *you!*

Yet I sense so many women walking around in an endless circle of fear and confusion, without wonder.

Have you lost your wonder?

When you lose your wonder, you lose your bravery. But when you live in the wonder of being the best of God's good work, then you understand that your days are ordained and written in God's story *before* you step into them and live them out.

There's an ordination to your life, a call already there at birth—your birthright gift ready for you to receive by simply agreeing with God that you were called to an acceptance, anointing, and appointing on this earth for His glory.

When you lose the wonder of that calling and that purpose, then your bravery and willingness to use your voice and become visible also become lost. The good news is that all will be restored.

The words of Revelation pull us into this stunning picture of a new garden and a new beginning. Someday, we will be restored to walk in complete acceptance, with an anointing and appointed destiny over our lives.

I believe that the new garden will not only be the end of our earthly journey, but also the start of something stunning, with fearless joy beating in every second. There will be the complete absence of fear and an opportunity for us to live as bravely ever.

> *Then I saw "a new heaven and a new earth," for the first heaven and the first earth had passed away, and there was no longer any sea. I saw the Holy City, the new Jerusalem, coming down out of heaven from God, prepared as a bride beautifully dressed for her husband. And I heard a loud voice from the throne saying, "Look! God's dwelling place is now among the people, and he will dwell with them. They will be his people, and God himself will be with them and be their God. 'He will wipe every tear from their eyes. There will be no more death or mourning or crying or pain, for the old order of things has passed away.*
> —Revelation 21:1–4, NIV

This means that Eve's worst choice on her worst day, Sarah's desire to control her situation by taking matters into her own hands, Leah and

Rachel's envy of each other's success, and Bathsheba's loss of power when David took her as his own will all be forgotten. The potential to even be motivated by anything other than the brave, risk-taking love of God won't exist.

Instead, you'll breathe in the sweet fragrance of favour for finishing well. You'll have proof in heaven that brave choices made on earth *matter*. The fragrance will be infused with the lingering scents of women's bravery. You'll be reminded of Eve persevering, even in her failure, of Sarah delivering Isaac as the promise of future generations in her old age, of Leah the "unlovely" and unloved, being chosen to bear the twelve tribes of Israel whose line led directly to Jesus, of Jochebed and Rahab surrendering bravely in *kairos* moments, of Ruth's valour, and of Bathsheba's brave voice speaking truth to power when she reminded David that her son, Solomon, must be the next king.

Your own brave story will be added to the intoxicating mix. *You* will be talked about in the halls of the mansions and the streets of pure gold.

The bravery of biblical women gave them the opportunity to be written into the story thread linking their lives to yours. There is an arrow shooting into the future that bears the potent ingredient of bravery from the first woman to your bravery, to the bravery of the women following after you. That arrow links us all and will propel us home.

Will you be caught up in the brave arrow's breathtaking momentum, linking you to all the women coming behind you, as your story finds its mark for generations to come?

Nothing will change unless you say "yes." Nothing will change unless you believe that your "yes" matters. Nothing will change unless you believe yourself brave, with the opportunity to make bold moves. Nothing will change unless you choose courage in a culture asking you to conform. You have the Holy Spirit to enable you to do things that are possible only with His power. Yours is to do what you can do, but first, you have to be brave enough to say "yes." And then you must let God do what only He can do—and watch what happens.

What a privilege it is that He's coming alongside you as you focus on a beautiful brave finish! So, how will you finish strong?

YOU NEED A CLEAR FOCUS

In a culture asking us to be *all* things to *all* people, it's no wonder that we not only lose our way, but we also lose our ability to distinguish between what our strong "yes" should be and what our strong "no" should be. When we're constantly tired of meeting the daily demands of life, being brave or creating space in our life to hear God's voice inviting us to step out in courage is often the last thing on our minds.

How do you become clear enough to create space to live bravely?

Maybe you've been saying "yes" to so much lately that you feel like a coward if you begin to say "no." But the opposite is true! The brave ones have learned the art of "no."

Here's a checklist of what to ask yourself the next time you're asked to take on a new responsibility:

- Is this consistent with my values and priorities?
- Is this within my area of unique giftedness and ability?
- Can someone else do it better?
- Can I delegate to someone else?
- What do my trusted friends say?
- Do I have the time?

Remember: There's something God has for you to do that only *you* can do.

So often, we get stuck doing what we're competent at, or even what we're excellent at. Even if you do something really well, if you can teach someone else to do it, you should, so that you can move into your area of unique ability, where only *you* can do that "thing." This is a place that only *you* can fill—no one else. When you're immersed in your area of unique ability, people will look at you and wonder, "How does she do it?" It will take bravery for you to lay something down in order to pick up something greater.

MY Q~ UNIQUE ABILITY	
UNIQUE ABILITY	EXCELLENT
COMPETENT	INCOMPETENT

I used to be a fundraiser and event planner. Many people told me that this was my gift, something I excelled at. I remember the night everything changed for me. I was sitting in the room at a fundraiser I had organized for a ministry I was working with. When the main speaker got on the platform to bring an inspiring message about why people should give, I suddenly realized, in that moment, that I no longer wanted to be the person organizing the event. I wanted to be the woman on the platform with the message!

Over the next few years, I worked with God in moving into that sweet spot where I could be Cathie, the woman with a message—instead of Cathie, the woman who organized the events where *others* would bring the message. This is one of the boldest moves I've ever made because the fear was that I would always be seen as the "fundraiser" or "event planner."

I learned that when I changed my dance steps, others had to change their steps in response to mine. It wasn't until I saw that I had something unique to offer to the world, and step into that with confidence, that others were able to see it in me, as well.

Is there an area of unique ability that you sense God has given you, and He's calling you to step into? What will it take for you to delegate, or gift, your current responsibilities to someone else in order to pursue the space designed uniquely for you to fill?

YOU NEED A COURAGEOUS FIGHT

When you decide to live by the courage of your convictions and use your voice to take a stand for what really matters, it will cost you. Know what you are prepared to live and die for.

I can't imagine living my life without raising my hand on behalf of the women in this nation who are finding encouragement and community through Gather Women. I plan to fight for the voice of women to find increased opportunities to gather and to be equipped in their gifting for the benefit of others locally, nationally, and globally. I plan to keep working on proclaiming the message that the local church has an opportunity to invite *half its constituents* into service in order for the larger church in Canada to flourish. I plan to keep investing in the soil God has planted me in.

When Jill Briscoe took the platform at the Just Give Me Jesus revival I mentioned earlier, she said, "Your mission field is the space between your two feet."

This is my mission field. This is my soil.

It's hard soil in so many ways. Women are spread out in this nation, and the work of calling women together so we can hear each other's words is challenging. There's a financial cost and an investment of time and energy. It's hard soil because Canada is the most multicultural country in the world, and the nations have gathered here in all of their beauty and diversity.

This isn't an accident; I believe it's by God's design.

What's on my watch to be part of transformation in this complex environment? The cost of figuring out how to create a place of beauty and belonging for women from diverse cultural, denominational, generational, and geographical backgrounds can't be understated. I believe, deep inside, that women, the church, our nation, and the world are worth the investment.

FIGHT FOR YOUR IDENTITY

Take time to explore what it means to have inherent value as a daughter of the King of the universe and to unpack your birthright gifts. It begins by looking at God and noticing how God is looking at you. If you are not clear on who you are, others will define it for you.

FIGHT FOR YOUR VALUES

Spend time with a values list and begin to choose the top 5 values that you are prepared to live and die for. My top value is stewardship so everything I take in I am compelled to give out. I will go to the wall to ensure not only I, but those God has entrusted me to influence, live to their full godly potential.

FIGHT FOR YOUR VISION

We spend more time planning birthday parties or vacations than we do planning our own lives. If you were running for office and making promises for the next four years, would you know what those would be, and would you vote for yourself? Have you considered crafting a mission statement for your life that can help you choose what you will say yes to and what you will say no to? Will you take time to create the picture of where you are headed and keep your focus and commit to finish strong?

YOU NEED A CONFIDENT FINISH

The most important principle that will get you to the finish line is knowing that *there's no way you can get there on your own.* Only by the power of the Holy Spirit can you do what God's asking of you. Philippians 4:13 reminds us: *"I can do all this through him who gives me strength"* (NIV).

His power is greater than any giant of fear you're facing. His power is greater than anything you feel you're lacking.

When Moses met God at the burning bush, he didn't need to remind God that he didn't have the courage or ability to go back and free His people from slavery. That's when God reminded Him, that He Himself, the *I AM*, would go with him and "do the thing" with Moses.

You never, ever have to go it alone. There are always two of you on the path to bravery—you and Jesus. He'll never ask you to do anything on your own. Your strength comes from Him, and Him alone. When you want to quit, you're asking Jesus to quit. When you say "no" to stepping out in bravery, you're asking Jesus to step back with you. Don't step back.

Step *forward*. He holds your hand. There's something about taking a leap of faith, holding hands with someone else that makes it safer, doesn't it?

Stay the path, friend. Don't quit. *Ever*. Jesus will be with you to help you bring your brave home.

I beg you,
take courage.
The brave soul can mend even disaster.

—Catherine the Great

CONCLUSION

Where Does Bravery Ever Get You?

I've noticed two different directions that many Christians, churches, denominations, and faith-based organizations across Canada take when it comes to women being welcomed (or not) into the fold of Christian leadership. Some are recognizing and embracing the change in having more women feel represented in the church narrative; for others, there's a resistance, at the senior leadership level, to inviting women into the roles of shepherding and leading.

As women ourselves, we might still be prone to yield to tradition and hierarchy, rather than taking the risk to be catalysts in reshaping the system in which we find ourselves.

How you will respond will depend on what you believe, and understanding what and who have shaped your beliefs. Perhaps a new definition of leadership is needed to open the door to new possibilities for you.

> If a theology of leadership is developed based on the model of the servant leadership of Christ, rather than on hierarchy and authority, there will be no theological problem with women responding to the call of God upon their lives and participating in any kind of ministry. When ministry is recognized as being in the Word rather than in the person, there will be no problem with the hermeneutical issues for the inconsistencies are all explainable within the broader context.[48]

There's a deep and wide blue ocean—or an open space free of competition—that's waiting to be filled with the stories of women who chose, and are choosing, to be culture shapers, definers, and transformers. That blue ocean is waiting for your unique story. You alone are the best qualified to speak of the faithfulness of God amid your most formidable battles. Perhaps the brave move awaiting you isn't launching a national ministry or preaching to a crowd. It could very well be having the courage to share your personal story, one word, one sentence, one paragraph at a time, for the glory of God.

What do you need to believe about your call to serve the church by developing and using your birthright gifts? How much more can we accomplish by encouraging and championing one another in our places of service? Do you believe that God can call you, not despite the fact that you are a woman, or because you are a woman, but because He has gifted you uniquely? Whom do you need to champion you?

Gather Women exists partly to do just that! We want to be a movement of women not only cheering you on from the sidelines, but also stepping on the track with you and running alongside you to the finish line.

> ... I lament that we are still arguing over whether women can teach, preach, and lead. We need to embolden women to ride the wave of the Spirit. We can't sit and hope it happens—we need to coach, train, cheer and empower women to catch the wave. If we aren't intentional about including, emboldening, equipping, training, and empowering those who are often excluded (women), there will hardly be a shift in the church's practice.[49]

How can we acknowledge that we are broken and often work against each other rather than together, and yet choose to believe that we are called to extraordinary lives partnering with God in His purposes?

Just as significantly, it helps to remember that our courage to be visible and bring our full gifts to our spheres of influence is for the benefit of serving others—all others. Both men and women. We are truly meant to flourish alongside each other, and so we are better together.

Where did bravery ever get you? How brave are you right now? Where will bravery get you in your future?

I want to share the following from Lynn Smith's writing, because I believe that her words have given shape and momentum to my obedience to God's call on my life.

The Great Commission was given to the church as a whole which includes women as well as men. The Holy Spirit equips women as well as men with whatever gifts are needed to "make disciples, teach and baptize." That equipping, whether it be in the area of leadership, teaching, or ministry will include authority but it will not be authority "over" another but the authority "of" the Word and Spirit of God. Consequently:

- Gifts are not gender-related
- Specific calling is not determined by gender
- Biology is not destiny; spiritual commitment is. True blessedness is open to single women and childless women as well as married women and men.
- God intended a unity when He created male and female.
- True unity negates hierarchy.
- Love, not legality is the measure of God's followers.[50]

I truly believe that true bravery is from love, for love, and activated by obedience. The desire to serve God and serve others is the catalyst to our bold moves whatever season we are in and whatever circumstances we find ourselves in.

I had a conversation with my friend and author, Jenni Catron, in which we were discussing the seasons of a woman leader's life—specifically *my* season. She encouraged me that I had "lots of runway left!" I fully intend to take up every inch of that runway before I turn off my engines.

But I don't want to fly that runway by myself and for myself. I have nothing to prove and nothing to lose. I want to soar to serve the entire body of Christ, both men and women. Whether the metaphor that works for you is a runway, a racetrack, or an ocean, there is ground to take and there are deep waves to ride. Are you in the middle of where the action is, or are you a spectator on the shore?

The kingdom of Jesus beckons men and women alike to ride the waves together, cheering one another on, coaching one another, and using their own talents to sharpen others. The church is hardly emboldened when over half of its members are standing on the shore. In the emboldened church all are participating, and all are riding the waves of the Spirit.[51]

How about you? Is the runway of your life waiting to have tracks branded on it that will be imprinted for eternity and serve as a landmark for those women and girls travelling in your wake? Maybe just one girl will hear about how you uniquely chose bravery; it just might change everything for her. The context of the past, in which the bravery of women was highlighted in the biblical narrative, informs our present so we can influence the future.

We live in a day and age when women's voices are rising to challenge the lack of gender equity in arenas of pay in the marketplace, social justice, and oppressed cultures. There's a resonant voice rising in the church, considering whether it's time for an equality of opportunity, opening up the possibility of more women to bring their full gifting to the body of Christ.

Dr. Pam MacRae has taught hundreds of women taking biblical studies at Moody Bible Institute. I resonate with her words:

> More than a few women seem to have a fear that any misstep will mean the lines of available ministry within the church will be drawn even more exclusively so as to push them further to the fringe by not allowing or inviting them into places of ministry or service. It can feel risky on both sides for women to engage fully. Honest conflict hovers around as women wonder if they are giving too much while leadership wonders if they are allowing too much.[52]

Context issues are the core of the conversations surfacing. Perhaps you've asked yourself one of the following questions:

- What's my place in the church? Lisa, a senior pastor, shared at the "Lydia's Daughters" conference, "My biggest lament is not being called a 'real' pastor, because I am a woman."
- Do I belong here?
- Can I have influence?

- Is there a glass ceiling or a red line above me? At the "Lydia's Daughters" gathering, a woman named Judith, who had been in ministry for fifty years, said, "I'm looking not at a glass ceiling, but at a cement ceiling."
- If I do invest in training and development, will there be a place for me to serve? A 2016 survey by ATS showed that "male M.Div. graduates remain more likely than female graduates to receive a job offer by the time of degree completion."[53]

It's not only the women asking the questions. For both men and women senior pastors or leaders in their churches, it can be a minefield.

> *Baffling* is a good word for it. It can be confusing for pastors who are open to women doing more in their churches but find there is this invisible barrier to recruiting and retaining high-quality female leaders. What is it? If we clearly have needs that a female leader could fill and we have qualified women available, what is the holdup?[54]

The questions have changed over the centuries, but what stays the same for all women of all time is the call to *character*. When we read the stories of biblical women, we're drawn deeper into the character issues that propelled them into their brave moments, despite the contexts of their day. Our character defines us and determines our life-altering choices. Character overrides context when God calls unlikely women to participate in life-changing destiny and purpose-filled moments.

Perhaps your definition of bravery needs to be expanded to include that the root of all bravery is simple obedience. It is responding to the call of God, however that looks for each of you. It is not based on how big the "thing" is that you do, but how wide your hands are open in surrender to His will.

I love these words from Jennie Catron:

> It is and it isn't about what we do. Our God-given influence isn't all about what we do, and yet we do have a purpose to accomplish. We don't do to earn God's love or acceptance or approval,

but we do as a response to the love and grace God has freely given us. We do out of love rather than out of obligation. Our doing is a response of thankfulness to God's doing in our lives."[55]

Our bravery is an obedient response to God's call. The circumstances might often be less than perfect, but our response can always be borne out of our faith in His goodness and our faith in His ability to do what He says He will do.

My prayer is that this book will act as a catalyst for you to step out in courage in your world, particularly if you're in a circumstance that is challenging and your fear is heightened.

It will look different for each of you, depending on where you find yourself. Maybe you are called to start a prayer ministry. Step out and do it! The seeds of opposition, sometimes invisible, usually sprout when the call on your life is to step into leadership in a church or ministry, or step into roles that involve teaching, preaching, and pastoring. Do you have the courage to still believe that you are called not because of your gender, but because of your giftedness?

My friend and mentor, Lynn Smith, was one of the first women to influence my understanding of the "gender or giftedness" tension.

A place to begin creating a vision for how women are to function in the church is by asking, "What would the church look like if it built ministry around gifts?" [as opposed to gender]. What structures best suit the message that the Holy Spirit has called men and women to live in a community of believers and has gifted those men and women to build up one another into Christ as the head?[56]

I hope that you, friend, will sense you're standing on the shoulders of brave women who have come before you, whose stories God included in the history and (her)story of how He called His people, men and women alike, to be part of His plan of redemption.

Modern women are looking for heroines to emulate in a world where God-honouring models of courage of hard to find. *You* are that woman! Do you believe that?

Perhaps these are your questions:

- How brave is brave?
- What would brave look like for me?
- How can I make my own bold move?

We've come full circle—from the beginning, with God making way for our brave by being the bravest Himself, through the middle, which is where we are now in our story, and to the end, where we will all end our brave story in glory with Jesus.

We've looked at stories of brave women in biblical times. We've read stories of brave women living today in our culture and are inspired by their bold moves. What is *your* story? Do you believe that you can have a new story and that it's being written right now?

We read in Revelation 2:17,

To everyone who is victorious I will give some of the manna that has been hidden away in heaven. And I will give to each one a white stone, and on the stone will be engraved a new name that no one understands except the one who receives it. (NLT)

This is promised to you.

How would you finish the sentence, "in my new story, I am…"? Do you believe that you can co-author your beautiful finish with God? Please be reminded of some of these foundational, powerful, and inspiring truths from Scripture to imagine where your journey of bravery will get you:

Trust in the Lord with all your heart, and do not lean on your own understanding.

—Proverbs 3:5, ESV

He said, "Come." So Peter got out of the boat and walked on the water and came to Jesus.

—Matthew 14:29, ESV

And the Lord said to me, "Arise, go on your journey at the head of the people, so that they may go in and possess the land, which I swore to their fathers to give them." And now, Israel, what does the Lord your God require of you, but to fear the Lord your God, to walk in all his ways, to love him, to serve the Lord your God with all your heart and with all your soul.

—Deuteronomy 10:11–12, ESV

For God gave us a spirit not of fear but of power and love and self-control.

—2 Timothy 1:7, ESV

Have I not commanded you? Be strong and courageous. Do not be frightened, and do not be dismayed, for the Lord your God is with you wherever you go.

—Joshua 1:9, ESV

I began this book by praying that you would lean into the lessons that come from studying the lives of women who lived in the past and those in your present. I continue to pray wholeheartedly that you will begin to see yourself in at least one of their stories.

As you look around you, you'll begin to notice brave women choosing, like you, to say what needs to be said and to do what needs to be done when the moment comes. You will know when it's time to choose brave and make your bold move. The Holy Spirit will prompt you. Be open to the moment when He says: "This is your *kairos* moment. Step into it."

Hear His words to you at this moment: *"For I am the Lord your God who takes hold of your right hand and says to you, Do not fear; I will help you"* (Isaiah 41:13, NIV).

There's a cloud of women witnesses who forged the path for you by their example. You can step out with courage and clear the path for all those coming after you.

Be brave. Choose courage. Don't conform. Your bold moment awaits you.

 SUCCESS IS NEVER FINAL;
FAILURE IS NEVER FATAL.
IT'S COURAGE THAT COUNTS.

APPENDIX

A BRAVE WOMAN'S DECLARATION

I declare, in Jesus' name, that I'm brave enough to allow You to free me from:

- The stranglehold of focusing on what I can't have
- The stranglehold of wanting something so desperately and then blaming You when it doesn't come to fruition in my *chronos* time
- The stranglehold of envy and wanting what others have, especially those closest to me
- The stranglehold of comparison and parading my good fortune in front of others
- The stranglehold of fear, especially when You ask me to risk everything by placing my most precious possession in a basket and surrendering it
- The stranglehold of my shame that keeps me from displaying the red cord of your salvation
- The stranglehold of the "to-do" list of the Proverbs 31 woman
- The stranglehold of my need to be constantly affirmed and valued
- The stranglehold of earthly success, which leaves me susceptible to sin

Instead, I receive the robes of righteousness measured just for me with the brave grace of Jesus. My bravery gives me:

- Abundance with measure in place of scarcity
- All that is mine in Jesus Christ
- All that will come to me if I wait in *kairos* time
- All that I can become in the presence of my closest rivals
- All that I stand to gain by "getting my brave on"
- All that I can leave for future generations as I put on my mantle of valour
- All that generations to come will be influenced by as I choose to move from success to significance, girded in strength and with my warrior armour on
- All the righteousness I am covered with as I confess my sin, in Jesus' name

ENDNOTES

1 Rosalie de Rosset, *Unseduced and Unshaken: The Place of Dignity in a Young Woman's Choices*, (Chicago, IL: Moody Publishers, 2012), 90.

2 Ibid.

3 Karoline M. Lewis, *She: Five Keys to Unlocking the Power of Women in Ministry*, (Nashville, TN: Abingdon Press, 2016), 82.

4 de Rosset, *Unseduced and Unshaken*, 85.

5 Lucy Peppiatt, *Rediscovering Scripture's Vision for Women*, (IVP ACADEMIC, August 6, 2019), 20.

6 Definition of *ezer kenegdo*: https://ezerkenegdo.org/ezer-kenegdo

7 de Rosset, *Unseduced and Unshaken*, 51.

8 Carolyn Custis James, *Half the Church: Recapturing God's Global Vision for Women*, (Grand Rapids, MI: Zondervan Press, 2011), 41.

9 *Kairos* (Ancient Greek: καιρός) is an Ancient Greek word meaning the right, critical, or opportune moment. The ancient Greeks had two words for time: *chronos* (χρόνος) and *kairos*. The former refers to chronological or sequential time, while the latter signifies a proper or opportune time for action. https://en.wikipedia.org/wiki/Kairos.

10 Definition of *brave*: https://www.merriam-webster.com/dictionary/brave

11 "Pliny the Elder Quotes." (n.d.). BrainyQuote.com. Accessed September 22, 2019. https://www.brainyquote.com/quotes/pliny_the_elder_120362

12 Kenneth Cooper, "How Immeasurable Is God?," *Journal of Dispensational Theology*, Vol. 13, No. 40 (December 2009), 48.

13 A. W. Tozer, *The Knowledge of the Holy*, (San Francisco, CA: HarperOne, 2009), vii.

14   Tozer, *The Knowledge of the Holy*, 1.

15   Ibid.

16   Marva J. Dawn, *To Walk and Not Faint: A Month of Meditations on Isaiah 40*, 2nd ed. (Grand Rapids, MI: William B. Eerdmans Publishing Company, 1997), 72.

17   Jennie Nadeau

18   Ted Loder, *Guerillas of Grace: Prayers for the Battle*, (Minneapolis, MN: Augsburg Books, 2004), 60–62.

19   Morgan Harper Nichols. www.morganharpernichols.com

20   Sue Monk Kidd, *When the Heart Waits: Spiritual Direction for Life's Sacred Questions*, (San Francisco, CA: HarperOne, 2016), 43.

21   Definition of *waiting*: https://www.lexico.com/en/definition/waiting

22   Jenni Catron, *Clout: Discover and Unleash Your God-Given Influence*, (Nashville, TN: Thomas Nelson, 2014), 199.

23   Alexander Solzhenitsyn. https://www.goodreads.com/quotes/415498-what-about-the-main-thing-in-life-all-its

24   Sue Monk Kidd, *The Secret Life of Bees*, (London, UK: Penguin Books, 2003), 96.

25   Catron, *Clout*, 39.

26   Adapted from Henri Nouwen, *Life of the Beloved*, 10th anniversary ed. (New York, NY: Crossroad Publishing, October 1, 2002).

27   Helen Keller. https://www.goodreads.com/quotes/9605-life-is-either-a-daring-adventure-or-nothing-at-all

28   Joanna Lafleur

29   Brené Brown, *Daring Greatly: How the Courage to Be Vulnerable Transforms the Way We Live, Love, Parent, and Lead*, (New York, NY: Avery Publishing, reprinted 2015), 1.

30   Bobbie Houston, "Things That Never Grow Old," Colour Conference, New York City, May 2017.

31   Soren Kierkegaard. https://www.goodreads.com/quotes/15578-to-dare-is-to-lose-one-s-footing-momentarily-not-to

32   J. R. R. Tolkien, *The Hobbit*. https://www.goodreads.com/quotes/96664-go-back-he-thought-no-good-at-all-go-sideways

33   Vanessa Hoyes

34   Rachel Held Evans, "3 Things You Might Not Know About Proverbs 31." RachelHeldEvans.com. Accessed September 18, 2019. https://rachelheldevans.com/blog/3-things-you-might-not-know-about-proverbs-31.

35   Jewish Women's Archive. "Eshet Chayil" (original text). https://jwa.org/node/23712. Accessed August 29, 2019.

36   Held Evans, "3 Things You Might Not Know About Proverbs 31"1

37   Definition of *gird*: https://www.vocabulary.com/dictionary/gird

38   Definition of *strength*: https://www.vocabulary.com/dictionary/strength

39   Chart adapted from Robert Steinke, "Healthy Congregations," 2nd ed. (Lanham, Rowman & Littlefield Publishing Group, November 20, 2006), 103–104.

40   Angela Duckworth, *Grit: The Power of Passion of Perseverance*, (New York, NY: Scribner, reprinted 2018), chapter 7.

41   Maggie Kuhn. https://quotefancy.com/quote/1281598/Maggie-Kuhn-Leave-safety-behind-Put-your-body-on-the-line-Stand-before-the-people-you

42   Kallie Wood. To learn more about her story and our Canadian history as it relates to First Nations people, visit www.convergingpathways.ca

43   Christine Caine, *Unexpected: Leave Fear Behind, Move Forward in Faith, Embrace the Adventure* (Grand Rapids, MI: Zondervan Press, 2018), 14.

44   Bonnie Pue

45   Thomas Merton, *New Seeds of Contemplation*, (New York, NY: New Directions, 1961) 256.

46   Dan Green. https://finishstrong.com/7-finish-strong-quotes/

47   Lynn Smith, *Gender or Giftedness: A Challenge to Rethink the Basis for Leadership Within the Christian Community*, A Study on the Role of Women, 2nd ed. (Long Beach, CA: Whitehorn Publishing, 2009, The World Evangelical Fellowship Commission on Women's Concerns, March 2000), 142.

48   Smith, *Gender or Giftedness*, 105.

49   Tara Beth Leach, *Emboldened: A Vision for Empowering Women in Ministry*, (Westmont, IL: InterVarsity Press, 2017), 184.

50   Smith, *Gender or Giftedness*, 110–111.

51   Leach, *Emboldened*, 185.

52   Dr. Pam MacRae, "Finding Your Voice," *Unseduced and Unshaken*, 2nd ed. (Chicago, Moody Publishers, 2012), 43.

53   ChristianCentury.com. Accessed October 30, 2018. https://www. christiancentury.org/article/news/report-details-trends-us-women-clergy.

54   Kadi Cole, *Developing Female Leaders*, (Nashville, TN: Thomas Nelson, 2019), 2.

55   Catron, *Clout*, 199.

56   Smith, *Gender or Giftedness*, 103.

ABOUT THE AUTHOR

 Cathie Ostapchuk is a speaker, leadership development trainer, consultant, and coach. Her work has included collaborations with global non-profit organizations, such as World Vision and Compassion Canada, and has taken her across Canada and as far as Africa and Australia doing the work she loves.

She is a lifelong learner and has studied at Moody Bible Institute, Biola University, University of Alberta, Tyndale Seminary, and Briercrest Seminary and holds two degrees as well as a Master's in Leadership and Management. Cathie is the co-founder and Lead Catalyst of Gather Women (gatherwomen.com). She co-hosts the HerInfluence podcast.

Cathie is committed to raising the profile and presence of Canadian Christian women coast to coast, believing that gathering, equipping, mobilizing, and championing Canadian Christian women will nurture a collective voice and a presence that can radically impact our churches, communities, and culture. You can find her at cathieostapchuk.com.